DISCOVERY IN FILM

Robert Heyer, S.J.   Anthony Meyer, S.J.

Designed by Emil Antonucci   Discovery Series Director: Richard J. Payne

Paulist Press
Paramus, N.J./New York, N.Y.
and
Association Press
New York, N.Y.

CONTENTS

GENERAL ACKNOWLEDGMENTS

Dr. Sidney Pleskin, Yeshiva University.

Jack McSherry, S.J.

Caroline Sugg, Lynn Lioio, Joseph Donohue, Joseph Scott, and Tom Sheehan.

Lawrence Ciske, Nick Mele, Robert Hilbert, Dominic Iocco and other students of Regis High School and Fordham Preparatory School.

Peter Courtney, Canadian film distribution

ACKNOWLEDGMENTS: READINGS

R. Houghton, *The Holiness of Sex*
Abbey Press
St. Meinrad, Indiana

J. T. Gilbert, S.J., *"Advertising Enterprise: The Art and Science"*
Advertising Enterprise
3700 Westline Boulevard
St. Louis, Missouri

J. McCall, S.J., *"A Pearl of a Girl"*
Argus Communications Company
3505 North Ashland Avenue
Chicago, Illinois

"In The Name of God"
John Secondari, Executive Producer of the *"Saga of Western Man"* Series American Broadcasting Company
Ave Maria Press
Notre Dame, Indiana

"We're Scared of Our Kids"
Ladies' Home Journal
Curtis Publishing Company
641 Lexington Avenue
New York, N.Y.

G. Bach, *"We Can Close the Generation Gap"*
Institute of Group Psychotherapy
450 North Bedford Drive
Beverly Hills, California

R. Fein, *"An Economic and Social Profile of the Negro American"*
Daedalus
7 Linden Street
Cambridge, Massachusetts

St. Exupery, *The Little Prince*
Harcourt, Brace & World, Inc.
757 Third Avenue
New York, N.Y.

Carl Sandburg, *"The People Will Live On"*
Harcourt, Brace & World, Inc.

A New Catechism: "Death," "The Scriptures and the Power of God," "Church in the World"
Herder and Herder, 1967
232 Madison Avenue
New York, N.Y.

Very Rev. Pedro Arrupe, S.J., *"Letter Addressed to Western Catholic Education Association Administrators Conference"*
Rev. Donald Montrose, S.J.
Jesuit Educational Quarterly
1717 Massachusetts Avenue
Washington, D.C.

"Prejudice South Africa"
Maryknoll Publications
Maryknoll, New York

Three quotes from R. Racine
Mass Media Ministries
2116 North Charles Street
Baltimore, Maryland

James Baldwin, *The Fire Next Time*
The Dial Press, Inc.
750 Third Avenue
New York, N.Y.

Pope Paul VI, *"Address to a General Audience on March 27, 1968"*
NC News Service
1312 Massachusetts Avenue, N.W.
Washington, D.C.

"Up From the Underground"
Newsweek
444 Madison Avenue
New York, N.Y.

Gerard Manley Hopkins, *"Hurrahing the Harvest"*
Poems of Gerard Manley Hopkins
Oxford University Press

Schulz, *Peanuts*
United Features Syndicate
220 East Forty-Second Street
New York, New York

J. O'Gara, *The Church and War*
National Council of Catholic Men
United States Catholic Conference
1312 Massachusetts Avenue, N.W.
Washington, D.C.

2 excerpts from the *New York Post*
The Associated Press
50 Rockefeller Plaza
New York, New York

Charles Chaplin, *Interview With Film Directors,* ed.
Andrew Sarris
Sight and Sound
London, England

Feature article on Andy Warhol
The News
220 East 42nd Street
New York, New York

P. Ochs, *"Changes"*
Barricade Music, Inc.
1697 Broadway, New York

Ingmar Bergman, INTERVIEWS WITH FILM DIRECTORS, ed. Andrew Sarris
Andrew Sarris
Cahiers du Cinema
12 West 9th Street
New York, New York

Donald Barr, *"Sex, Love and Modern Education,"*
COLUMBIA COLLEGE TODAY
Columbia University
New York, New York

A. Ginsberg, *"Who Be Kind To"*
Cranium Press
642 Shrader
San Francisco, California

John Updike, *"Hub Fans Bid Kid Adieu"*
Alfred A. Knopf, Inc.
501 Madison Avenue
New York, New York

W. H. Auden, *"The Unknown Citizen"*
Random House Inc., Alfred A. Knopf, Inc.
501 Madison Avenue
New York, New York

Margaret Mead, FAMILY
The Macmillan Company
60 Fifth Avenue
New York, New York

J. B. Phillips, NEW TESTAMENT IN MODERN ENGLISH
The Macmillan Company
60 Fifth Avenue
New York, New York

M. K. Gandhi, YOUNG INDIA
Navajivan Trust
Ahmedabad 14
Gujerat State
India

C. Brown, MANCHILD IN THE PROMISED LAND
New American Library
1310 Avenue of the Americas
New York, New York

"Thanatology"
Time Magazine
Rockefeller Center
New York, New York

Garret Hardin, *"Abortion—Or Compulsory Pregnancy?"*
JOURNAL OF MARRIAGE AND THE FAMILY
George Banta Publishing Company, Inc.
Minneapolis, Minnesota

Time Magazine—2 excerpts
Rockefeller Center
New York, New York

ACKNOWLEDGMENTS: PHOTOGRAPHY

FILM   **CREDIT**
Hunger in America: Carousel Films, Inc.
Christmas in Appalachia: Columbia Broadcasting System, Inc.
The Hand: United Nations
Hunger in America: Carousel Films, Inc.
Black and White in South Africa: United Nations
Harlem Wednesday: Storybord, Inc.
No Reason To Stay: National Film Board of Canada
Ginsberg and Ferlinghetti: NET Center
Days of Dylan Thomas: McGraw-Hill/Contemporary Films
Henry More: Wide World Photos
LSD: Insight or Insanity?: Bailey Films
The Seekers: New York State Narcotics Commission
World of Three: National Film Board of Canada
Adventures of an *: Storybord, Inc.
Place in the Sun: Schulz, United Features Syndicate
Ask Me, Don't Tell Me: Carl May, American Friends Service Committee
Viva La Calle 103: Wide World Photos
That's Me: McGraw-Hill/Contemporary Films
Inscape: St. Francis Production
The Detached American: Wide World Photos
The Hutterites: Wide World Photos
David and Hazel: National Film Board of Canada
A Trumpet for the Combo: National Film Board of Canada
Two Men and a Wardrobe: McGraw-Hill/Contemporary Films
The Most: United Nations
The Game: McGraw-Hill Films
Phoebe: National Film Board of Canada

FILM   **CREDIT**
Merry-Go-Round: McGraw-Hill Films
A Quarter Million Teenagers: Churchill Films, Inc.
You're No Good: National Film Board of Canada
Overture: United Nations
The Soldier: Vito Cioffero, Sign Magazine
The Nativity of Jesus Christ: Wide World Photos
Night and Fog: United Nations
Time Out of War: McGraw-Hill/Contemporary Films
Neighbors: National Film Board of Canada
The Hole: Storybord, Inc.
23 Skidoo: National Film Board of Canada
The Hat: Storybord, Inc.
Gandhi: Wide World Photos
A Divided World: Wide World Photos
Vivre: United Nations
Occurrence at Owl Creek Bridge: United Nations
Runner: National Film Board of Canada
Very Nice, Very Nice: National Film Board of Canada
Chartres: Wide World Photos
String Bean: Ewing Galloway
My Own Backyard To Play In: United Nations
21–87: United Nations
Road Signs on a Merry-Go-Round: Columbia Broadcasting System
Automania 2000: McGraw-Hill/Contemporary Films
World in a Marsh: United Nations
Prehistoric Images: Wide World Photos
The House: McGraw-Hill/Contemporary Films
Dodge City: New Line Cinema Corporation
Thanatopsis: Ed Emshwiller
Time of the Locust: Wide World Photos
Schmeerguntz: Ewing Galloway
Science Friction: Stan Vanderbeek
Leaf: Pyramid Film Production

LIST OF PRODUCERS AND DISTRIBUTORS

1 **AMERICAN FRIENDS SERVICE COMMIT-TEE**
160 N. 15th Street
Philadelphia, Pennsylvania 19102
2 431 S. Dearborn Street
Chicago, Illinois 60605
3 **ASSOCIATION FILMS, INC.**
600 Madison Avenue
New York, N.Y. 10022
also:
600 Grand Avenue, Ridgefield, N.J., 07657
324 Delaware Avenue, Oakmont, Pa. 15139
561 Hillgrove Avenue, LaGrange, Ill. 60525
1621 Dragon Street, Dallas, Texas 75207
25358 Cypress Avenue, Hayward, Calif. 94544
135 Peter Street, Toronto 2B, Ontario, Canada
Sales Office
400 N. Michigan Avenue, Chicago, Ill. 60611
4 **AUDIO FILM CENTER**
10 Fiske Place
Mount Vernon, N.Y. 10550
914–664–5051
also:
2138 E. 75th Street, Chicago, Ill. 60649
312–684–2531
406 Clement Street, San Francisco, Calif. 94118
415–751–8080
5 **BAILEY FILMS INC.**
6509 de Lengre Ave.
Hollywood, California 90028
6 **BALLENTINE, RICHARD**
Toronto
7 **BECKER, HAROLD**
8 **BRANDON FILMS INC.**
221 West 57th Street
New York, N.Y. 10019
212–246–4867

also:
FILM CENTER INC.
20 East Huron Street
Chicago, Illinois 60611
312–DE 7–2855
WESTERN CINEMA GUILD
244 Kearny Street
San Francisco, California 94108
415–EX 7–4255
9 **BRITISH INFORMATION SERVICE**
(cf. Contemporary)
10 **BROOKLYN PUBLIC LIBRARY FILM DEPT.**
Eastern Parkway
Brooklyn, N.Y.
11 **CANYON CINEMA COOPERATIVE**
58 Verona Place
San Francisco, California 94107
415–781–4791
12 **CAROUSEL FILMS INC.**
1501 Broadway
New York, N.Y. 10036
212–BR 9–6734
13 **CHURCHILL FILMS**
662 North Robertson Blvd.
Los Angeles, California 90069
14 **CINEMA 16 FILM LIBRARY**
80 University Place
New York, N.Y. 10003
212–989–6400
15 **COLUMBIA BROADCASTING SYSTEM**
51 West 52nd Street
New York, N.Y. 10019
212–765–4321
16 **COMO FILMS & ARGOS FILMS**
Cocinor, France
17 **CONTEMPORARY FILMS, INC.**

267 West 25th Street
New York, N.Y. 10001
212–971–6681
also:
614 Davis Street, Evanston, Ill. 60201
1211 Polk Street
San Francisco, California 94109

18 **ENCYCLOPEDIA BRITANNICA FILMS**
1150 Wilmette Avenue
Wilmette, Illinois
also:
425 N. Michigan Avenue, Chicago, Ill. 60611
4420 Oakton Street, Skokie, Ill. 60076
38 W. 32nd Street, New York, N.Y. 10001
26539 Grand River Rd., Detroit, Michigan 48240
5625 Hollywood Blvd., Hollywood, Calif. 90028
277 Pharr Road, N.E., Atlanta, Ga. 30305

19 **FAMILY THEATRE**
7201 Sunset Blvd.,
Hollywood, California 90046

20 **FILM MAKERS COOPERATIVE**
175 Lexington Avenue
New York, N.Y. 10016

21 **GEORGE K. ARTHUR
GO PICTURES**
37 West 57th Street
New York, N.Y.

22 **HALAS AND BACHELOR
CARTOON FILMS**
London, England

23 **JOHN HUBLEY**
(cf. Storyboard Inc., below)

24 **ICHAC, MARCEL**

25 **INTERNATIONAL FILM BUREAU**
332 S. Michigan Avenue
Chicago, Illinois 60604

26 **JANUS FILMS, INC.**
24 West 58th Street
New York, N.Y. 10019

212–PL3–7100

27 **MASS MEDIA MINISTRIES**
2116 North Charles Street
Baltimore, Maryland 21218
301–727–3270
also:
1714 Stockton Street
San Francisco, California 94133

28 **MC GRAW-HILL TEXT FILMS, INC.**
330 West 42nd Street
New York, N.Y. 10036
212–971–6681

29 **MC KENNA, ROLLIE**

30 **MEDICINE PRODUCTIONS**

31 **MUSEUM OF MODERN ART,
FILM DEPARTMENT**
11 West 53rd Street
New York, N.Y.
212–245–3200

32 **NATIONAL COUNCIL OF CATHOLIC
MEN FILM CENTER**
405 Lexington Avenue
New York, N.Y. 10017

33 **NATIONAL COUNCIL OF CHURCHES
OF CHRIST**
Broadcasting and Film Commission
475 Riverside Drive
New York, N.Y. 10027

34 **NATIONAL FILM BOARD OF CANADA**
680 Fifth Avenue
New York, N.Y. 10019
212–JU 6–2400

35 **N.E.T. FILM SERVICE**
Indiana University
Bloomington, Indiana

36 **NEW YORK PUBLIC LIBRARY
FILM CENTER
DONNELL LIBRARY CENTER**
20 West 53rd Street

New York, N.Y.
212–OX 5–4200

37 NEW YORK STATE NARCOTIC CONTROL COMMISSION ADMINISTRATIVE OFFICES
Stuyvesant Plaza
Albany, N.Y. 12203

38 NEW YORK UNIVERSITY FILM LIBRARY
26 Washington Place
New York, N.Y. 10003
212–SP 7–2000

39 PINTOFF, ERNEST

40 POLISH FILM UNIVERSITY

41 PYRAMID FILMS
P.O. Box 1048
Santa Monica, California 90406

42 QUEENS BOROUGH PUBLIC LIBRARY
89–11 Merrick Boulevard
Jamaica, New York 11432
212–RE 9–1900, Ext. 303

43 WALTER READE ORGANIZATION
241 East 34th Street
New York, N.Y. 10016
212–683–6300

44 RELIGIOUS FILMS

45 DE ROUBAIX, PAUL

46 SECONDARI, JOHN AND ROGERS, HELEN JEAN

47 SHEPPARD, GORDON
Toronto

48 SOLIN, MYRON

49 STERLING EDUCATIONAL FILMS
241 East 34th Street
New York, N.Y.

50 STORYBOARD, INC.
165 East 72nd Street
New York, N.Y.
212–744–8050

51 SUMMER IN THE CITY
32 East 51st Street

New York, N.Y.

52 SUSKDORSS, ARNIE

53 TRICKFILMS PRODUCTIONS
Prague, Holland

54 UNITED NATIONS
Office of Public Information
U.N. Plaza
New York, N.Y. 10017

55 UNITED WORLD FILMS, INC.
221 Park Avenue
New York, N.Y. 10003
212–777–6600
also:
287 Techwood Drive, N.W., Atlanta, Ga. 30313
542 S. Dearborn Street, Chicago, Ill. 60605
2227 Bryan Street, Dallas, Texas 75201
1025 N. Highland, Los Angeles, California 90038
5023 NE Sandy Blvd, Portland, Ore. 97213

56 UNIVERSITY OF CALIFORNIA
Educational Sales Department
U. of California, Extension
Berkeley 4, California

57 VILDARDEBO, CARLOS

58 WALKER PRODUCTIONS

59 WALTER READE ORGANIZATION
241 East 34th Street
New York, N.Y.
212–683–6300

60 WCAU-TV, PHILADELPHIA

61 YESHIVA UNIVERSITY
Film Library
526 West 187th Street
New York, N.Y. 10033
212–SW 5–6460

62 AMBASSADE DE FRANCE
42 Sussex Drive
Ottawa, Ontario

63 ASTRAL FILMS LIMITED

224 Davenport Road
Toronto 5, Ontario
Canada
924–9721

64 **AUDIO VISUAL SERVICES**
CENTRAL LIBRARY AUDIO VISUAL
SERVICES
220 College Street
Toronto 2B
Canada
927–3901

BOROUGH OF YORK AVS
1745 Eglinton Avenue West
Toronto 10
Canada
781–5208

EAST YORK AVS
Memorial Park and Durant Avenues
Toronto 6
Canada
425–8222

ETOBICOKE AVS—RICHVIEW
600 Islington Avenue North
Etobicoke
Canada
248–5681

ETOBICOKE AVS—NEW TORONTO
11th Street
New Toronto
Canada
259–3971

NORTH YORK AVS
5126 Young Street
Willowdale
Canada
225–8891

SCARBOROUGH AVS
545 Markham Road
Scarborough

Canada
266–1260

65 **ALCOHOLISM AND DRUG ADDICTION**
RESEARCH FOUNDATION
Education Division
344 Bloor Street West
Toronto 4, Ontario
Canada
365–4521

66 **ENCYCLOPAEDIA BRITTANICA**
PUBLICATIONS LIMITED
151 Bloor Street West
Toronto 5, Ontario
Canada
925–9531

67 **CANADIAN FILM-MAKERS'**
DISTRIBUTION CENTRE
719 Yonge Street
Toronto 5, Ontario
921–2259
as of January 1, 1969:
c/o Rochdale College
Bloor & Huron Streets
Toronto 5, Ontario
Canada

68 **CANADIAN FILM INSTITUTE**
1762 Carling Avenue
Ottawa 13, Ontario
Canada
729–6193

69 **EDUCATIONAL FILM DISTRIBUTORS**
LIMITED
191 Eglinton Avenue East
Toronto 12, Ontario
Canada
489–2314

70 **CENTRAL FILM LIBRARY**
Anglican Church House
600 Jarvis Street

Toronto 5, Ontario
924–9194

71 **FILM CANADA PRESENTATIONS LIMITED**
1 Charles Street East
Toronto 5, Ontario
922–4187

72 **INTERVIDEO PRODUCTIONS**
65 Front Street East
Toronto, Ontario
Canada
362–0442

73 **MR. A. MAGGIOROTTI c/o WARNER BROTHERS—SEVEN ARTS PICTURES DISTRIBUTING CO.**
70 Carlton Street
Toronto 2, Ontario
Canada
922–2692

74 **MC GRAW-HILL TEXT FILMS**
330 Progress Avenue
Scarborough, Ontario
Canada
293–1911

75 **OFFICE OF RELIGIOUS EDUCATION**
241 McRae Drive
Toronto 17, Ontario
Canada
421–8950

76 **UNITED CHURCH DISTRIBUTION SERVICE**
299 Queen Street West
Toronto 2B, Ontario
Canada
also:
District Service
509 Richards Street
Vancouver, British Columbia
District Service

Alberta Depot
Alberta College
1004–101st Street
Edmonton, Alberta
District Service
Winnipeg Depot
120 Maryland Street
Winnipeg, Manitoba

77 **NATIONAL FILM BOARD**
distribution offices:
BRITISH COLUMBIA
Vancouver: Room 415, 325 Granville Street
Abbotsford: 2469 Montrose Avenue (P.O. Box 1390)
Kelowna: 1561 Ellis Street
Nelson: Room 205, Federal Bldg., 514 Vernon Street
Prince George: Room 31, Federal Bldg., 1323 5th Avenue
Victoria: Room 308, 816 Government Street
SASKATCHEWAN
Saskatoon: Regional Office, Room 210, Federal Bldg., 1st Avenue and 22nd St.
Regina: Room 507, 5th Floor, New Post Office Bldg, South Railway Street
ALBERTA
Calgary: Room 713, Public Building
Edmonton: South Side Post Office Building
MANITOBA
Brandon: Room 205, Brandon Federal Building
Winnipeg: 1130 Ellice Avenue
ONTARIO
Toronto: Regional Office, Mackenzie Bldg, 1 Lombard Street
Fort William: c/o Fort William Public Library
Hamilton: National Revenue Bldg., Room 551, 150 Main Street West
Hanover: Federal Bldg., 9th Avenue
Kingston: Room 275, New Federal Bldg.,

Clarence Street
London: Income Tax Bldg., 388 Dundas Street
North Bay: Room 205, 101 Washington Avenue East
Orilla: 210 Federal Bldg., 17–25 Peter Street, N2 West
Ottawa: Excelsior Life Bldg., 270 Laurier Avenue West
QUEBEC
Montreal: Regional Office, 550 Sherbrooke Street West, Montreal 18
Chicoutimi: Federal Bldg., 222 Racine Street East
Hull-Ottawa: Excelsior Life Bldg., 270 Laurier Avenue West
Joliette: Post Office Bldg., 409 Notre Dame Street
Sherbrooke: Federal Bldg.
St.-Jean: 246 Champlain Street, Côté Bldg., P.O. Box 547
Trois Rivières: Room 300, Post Office Building
Quebec: Room 24, Palais Montcalm
Rimouski: 53 Cathedral Avenue, P.O. Box 850
NOVA SCOTIA
Halifax: Regional Office, 1572 Barrington Street
New Glasgow: Room 100, New Federal Bldg.
Sydney: Room 244, Federal Bldg., Dorchester Street
NEW BRUNSWICK
Bathurst: Veniot Bldg., 435 King Avenue, P.O. Box 10
Fredericton: Federal Bldg., P.O. Box 216
Moncton: Room 411, New Federal Bldg., P.O. Box 482
Saint Joan: Customs Bldg., P.O. Box 733
PRINCE EDWARD ISLAND

Charlottetown: Confederation Bldg.
NEWFOUNDLAND
Corner Brook: Barry-Wells-Doucette Bldg., 17 West Street, P.O. Box 51
St. John's: Bldg. 303, Fort Pepperell (P.O. Box 1206)

78 **MONDAY MORNING FILMS**
55 York Street
Toronto 1, Ontario

FOREWORD

Here is a book which offers an uncommon and stimulating guide to some short films that are available and useful as teaching aids for colleges and schools.

In this day when motion pictures are becoming more and more the cultural medium by which young people are most excited and to which teachers are learning to turn for assisting illumination, this volume eminently serves as a roadmap and guidebook through an area that has been sadly neglected by historians and analysts of films.

The short film has been a stepchild of the established motion picture industry ever since feature length films came to the fore as the dominant commercial merchandise. The short, except for cartoons and newsreels, was left largely to the marginal makers of documentary films and to independent enterprisers and promoters who had particular messages to convey. As a consequence, the tendency has been to neglect short films in the limited cinema liteurature.

But the short, meaning any film under more than one-hour feature-length, is a particularly viable item for instructional purposes. It is compact. Its ideas are usually simple and direct, not diffuse. And its running time is not excessive for the average student's interest-span. Furthermore, good shorts may be obtained for reasonable rental fees and are therefore peculiarly congenial to the budgets of hard-pressed colleges and schools.

Anthony Meyer and Robert Heyer have made an excellent selection of classic and unusual shorts, they have described their contents concisely, and aptly suggested discussion topics to stimulate thought. It is clear that they have not endeavored to restrict their range of suggested films to any narrow curricula channels, but have offered films that will be useful in several fields of conventional curriculum patterns and invite the teacher to use judgment in defining their possible use.

Beyond their importance for teaching, the films suggested here are eminent examples of artistry and craftmanship in the expanding field of cinema. The teacher or discussion leader who has some knowledge of the art and craft can make splendid use of these examples in illuminating the medium itself.

I am particularly happy that the authors have included several familiar films of the so-called "underground" which has been criticized or suspected by cautious observers of cinema in recent years. A great deal of very interesting experimental work has been done in this area of independent production, and the enterprising teacher can make good use in many ways, including the promotion of open-mindedness, of the several underground films suggested here.

Of course, this volume does not begin to scan the whole available treasury of short films. The thousands of items in existence would be too much for any one volume to contain. But catalogues with thumb-nail descriptions may be obtained from the distributing libraries listed in this book. And, again, the enterprising teacher can use these to proceed further on his own.

That is one of the "dividend" advantages of this handy book. It encourages exploration, which is the prelude to real Discovery.

Bosley Crowther

INTRODUCTION

Discovery in Film explores the use of short, non-feature films for educational purposes. It has in mind educators, particularly teachers of Theology and English in secondary schools and their counterparts in parishes and organizations who work with teenagers and adults in discussion situations. The book should prove helpful to psychology seminars, family discussion clubs and Christian doctrine and retreat groups.

Discovery in Film discusses seventy-eight non-feature films. Most of them have won major awards; all of them have been screened for their actual success in teaching situations. The emphasis of *Discovery in Film* is possibility—new approaches, new uses of film for education. *Soldier* suggests the use of film during religious ceremonies. The critique of *Two Men and a Wardrobe* includes a sequential outline of the film. *Window Water Baby Moving* and *Schmeerguntz* establish the Underground as a legitimate and accessible source of films. The discussion of *Chartres* and *The Sacrifice and the Resurrection* relates architecture to evolution. *Hutterites* raises the question of a closed society living within a world community. *Black and White in South Africa* presents the problem of apartheid. *The Hand* views the problem of fate; *House* the problem of time. *Ginsberg and Ferlinghetti* takes an inside look at offbeat contemporary poetry. Most critiques include related material to broaden the film's discussion potential.

Discovery in Film catalogs each film according to the five themes of the Discovery Series: Communication, Freedom, Love, Peace and Happiness—and the Underground. The standard critique presents each film from a fourfold perspective:

1 *COMMENT:* To communicate a general awareness of the film's content and style. When the camera technique, production background or plot structure of a film is of special significance or difficulty, an appropriate emphasis is given within the comment.
2 *DISCUSSION QUESTIONS:* To initiate discussion about the film. Depending on the nature of the film, these questions sometimes probe the concrete data of a specific sequence and sometimes relate the discussion to a theme not directly stated in the film.
3 *RESOURCE MATERIALS:* To broaden the discussion and workshop potential of each film. The resource material includes scenario outlines, interviews, poems, photographs, quotations, etc.
4 *DATA:* To list clearly the production background, major awards and exact rental availability of each film in the United States and Canada.

Discovery in Film has an Appendix which offers: (1) a brief presentation on three major propaganda films; (2) a selection of feature films classified according to the themes of the Discovery Series; (3) an essay on *Teaching the Film* which briefly suggests an approach to creative education through the film "term paper" and a course in film making; (4) a number of suggestions for the use of film in retreat situations; (5) an alphabetical index of the non-feature films discussed in the book.

DISCOVERY IN FILM

COMMUNICATION

Adventures of an*
Place in the Sun
Ask Me, Don't Tell Me
Viva La Calle 103
That's Me
Inscape
Lines Horizontal
The Detached Americans
Hutterites
David and Hazel
A Trumpet for the Combo
Sky
Leaf
Two Men and a Wardrobe
The Critic

ADVENTURES OF AN *

✠ is naturally proud of his son, *. * enjoys the world around him and one day builds a tree house using the front path flagstones for construction material.   ✠, tired and worn from a long day's work, stumbles over his absent path, tears the tree house down and leaves * alone to cry. As the years pass, * grows through the normal phases of adolescence and education until he settles into a job and home of his own. * also has a child, *2. *2 confronts his father with a large play-horse constructed out of scrap material on the front lawn. At first * is disturbed, but, unlike   ✠ , * decides to help *2. The horse becomes magically alive, and both * and *2 ride off into the distance, enjoying the wonders of life that * had by this time forgotten.

Adventures of an * is one of four John Hubley animated films presented in this book. Hubley is a master of animation and color. His films are always a pleasure to watch. In this particular film, Hubley discourages the suppression of wonder natural to youth and explores the relation between generations. *Adventures of an* * makes an entertaining point of departure for a discussion in either of these areas—the place of wonder in a logical society or the generation barrier.

How does * *cause* ✠ *anxiety? Does* ✠ *cause* * *anxiety?*

In what ways does ✠ *help or hinder* * *in his striving to grow? How would you encourage growth?*

How does * *conform to his friends, and how does this affect his growing independence?*

How is the art of painting presented in this film?

How does * *encourage* *2 *with his creativity?*

If there is a place for wonder in a logical world, in what way can it be developed? What does a growing child wonder about that leads to his growing?

Related material: refer to DISCOVERY IN SONG, Hair of Spun Gold, *page 67*

"Talking to my parents is a drag. They just pull age on you. There is never any real discussion."

"Kids today have no backbone. They say they're against the Vietnam War for moral reasons. I say they're scared."

"If there's one thing I can't stand it's when my father says, 'Take it from my experience.' The last thing that I want to be in 20 years is like him."

"Our kids have everything given to them. My generation had to work for what it got."

"I wish I could talk to my parents. If I were honest, I'd be grounded for two months. Parents are too narrow to be told anything."

"My son doesn't know enough to come in out of the rain. He isn't even clean. What right does he have to tell me I don't care about the suffering in the world?"

(*From G. Bach, "We Can Close the Generation Gap,"* Ladies' Home Journal, *Jan. 1968, p. 36*)

Scene from *Adventures of an**

WHO'S WINNING THE BATTLE OF THE GENERATION GAP?

The distressing news is that parents are retreating on almost all fronts—often in confusion and sometimes in sheer panic.

Many parents actually seem afraid of their children —afraid to discipline them, afraid of losing their love, afraid of losing face, afraid the kids will turn against them.

Many parents feel so guilty about their own shortcomings that they appear incapable of straightening out their children.

Many parents are so tyrannized by their children that they are not altogether sure that adults are still running the world.

Many parents appear too lazy to get involved with their children's problems.

Many parents are afraid to test their authority over their children. They don't want to be humiliated by seeing how little power parents really have.

Many parents feel powerless to bring up children properly because the world changes with such bewildering speed.

Many parents have the uneasy feeling that their children see right through them.

Many parents don't tell children the facts of life because they suspect the kids know more than they do.

Many parents can cope with children who are just like them—but are upset by children who are not.

Many parents are afraid of their children's questions for fear of exposing how little they know.

Many parents worry that if they are too lenient their children will turn out to be failures.

(*From* Ladies' Home Journal, *Jan. 1968, p. 5*)

ADVENTURES OF AN *

Storyboard, Inc.
1957

10 minutes, color, 16mm., animated

Purchase—$120.00 (#8); in Canada (#74)
Rental—$7.50 (#8, #17, #27, #42); in Canada (#68, #70)

Director: John Hubley
Writers: John Hubley and Faith Elliot in collaboration with James Johnson Sweeny
Animation: Emery Hawkins
Music: Benny Carter

Awards

Venice Film Festival Award 1957 (Excellence in field of 10 minute short subjects)
Montevideo Film Festival Award
Australian Film Festival Award
Tours Film Festival Award

Brussels International Experimental Film Festival
1958

PLACE IN THE SUN

The two animated characters in this film struggle with each other for a coveted piece of sunlight. The sunlight suddenly disappears, and the characters realize that only by their working together can the sun be made to return. The characters do work together, the sunlight returns and all ends well.

This clever cartoon is enjoyable for any age. Its discussion value is extremely limited, however, and the film has rather been used to stimulate experiments in "cartoon theology." "Cartoon theology" may be defined as a religious lesson conveyed through cartoon characters. It can be simply practiced by individuals or a group by arranging cartoon cutouts on paper or in a film to tell a "moral" story. Younger students seem to enjoy a hunt through magazines and comic books to find examples of cartoon theology, while older students seem to prefer shooting semi-animated eight millimeter films out of newspaper clippings. In either case, *Place in the Sun* is a good introductory film for a lesson in cartoon theology.

Have you ever experienced conflict that ended in a closer personal relationship?

What is the "place in the sun" for the American teenager? For the Indian American teenager? For the Black American teenager? For the Asian teenager? For the South American teenager? For the African teenager?

Do you think that it is typical for people when satisfied to look for something to argue about?

Some topics for original cartoons or short films:
Freedom is money.
Compulsory worship.
Forced discussion.
Dating practices (kissing, etc.).
Magic and sin.
Non-community community.
Sunday sermon.
Generation gap.
Hidden race prejudices (housing, jobs).
Style of living (hippie, etc.).

PLACE IN THE SUN

Trickfilms Productions
Prague, Holland
1960

8 minutes, color, 16mm., animated

Purchase: inquire (#21)
Rental: $15.50 (#10, #61)

Producer: Frantisek Vystrcil

ASK ME, DON'T TELL ME
and VIVA LA CALLE 103

Ask Me, Don't Tell Me is the story of a street gang in San Francisco. Its membership incorporates personnel from several formerly independent gangs. It is called Youth for Service, enrolling the toughest youth elements in San Francisco. The principle behind Youth for Service is "Ask me, don't tell me," the plea of youth to be included in the adult world,

30

to be asked to help, to be needed. The teenager is in a gang because of his desire for community, his need to work for status, his need to be needed. Youth for Service needs these teenagers. The gang is a neighborhood help organization which builds and paints and performs heavy work for those too old or unable to do it themselves. When the community wants something done, it calls on Youth for Service. It has replaced traditional suspicion by entrusting the gang with greater responsibility.

In the summer of 1967 in New York City, there were no riots in Spanish Harlem. A group of local residents and a Roman Catholic priest, Monsignor Robert J. Fox, went out into the street the night the riots were threatened. They began a street procession. Every night that week, against police warnings, they went into the street. The group became a singing fiesta-parade. Hundreds followed them. There were no riots.

East 103rd Street decided to go farther. They wished to bring their cares and their happiness and their sorrows into the street. It was *their* street, and living there, they seemed dispossessed of it. They would reclaim their street. 103rd Street invited a hundred suburbanites to help them. One September day the street was filled with "foreign" suburbanites and local Harlem residents. Truckloads of garbage were removed; the fronts of buildings were repainted; dinner and dancing and a fiesta spirit had been established in the street.

Today, 103rd Street is still clean. The city has given it trees. But more importantly, 103rd Street speaks on its own and has friends in many other neighborhoods. It is a desirable home for its residents. Since 103rd Street, Monsignor Fox has developed similar situations in a regular pattern in hundreds of other blocks. Some have succeeded; some have failed. *Viva La Calle 103* is the 103rd Street story.

It is a beautiful on-the-spot documentary of the famous 103rd Street fiesta clean-up day.

Youth for Service in San Francisco and Monsignor Fox in New York City contradict traditional community images. A gang and a ghetto street: desirable? capable of beauty? Youth for Service and Monsignor Fox prove that beauty is there and that its revelation is up to the community. They present a viable alternative to violence and suppression.

Ask Me, Don't Tell Me and *Viva La Calle 103* are films which should introduce audience self-appraisal. Are the members of the audience, their school or organization doing anything socially orientated? It is clearly possible to begin a community solution to racism, disunity and community disruption. It requires only the common man's ability to make friends, to ask for help, or simply to drink beer and dance. For a full picture of a project with this orientation, see *Summer in the City* by Mary Cole, with a Foreword by Monsignor Fox (P. J. Kenedy: New York, 1968).

What is the meaning and importance of service? What attitudes are necessary for true service?

What service organizations do you know of in your city? Search out some of the following and report on their programs of creative service. For example, here are some New York agencies and addresses:

National Conference of Christians and Jews (43 W. 57th St., N.Y., N.Y. 10019)

Volunteer Coordinating Council of New York City (250 Broadway, N.Y., N.Y. 10007)

National Association for the Advancement of Colored People (20 W. 40th St., N.Y., N.Y.)

Urban League (217 W. 125th St., N.Y., N.Y. 10027)

Department of Voluntary Service and Youth Ministry (475 Riverside Dr., N.Y., N.Y. 10027)

Catholic Interracial Council (N.Y. CIC 55 Liberty St., N.Y., N.Y. 10005)

Catholic Big Brothers (122 E. 22nd St., N.Y., N.Y.)

VIVA LA CALLE 103

Mark Statler, Pelican Films
1967

13 minutes, black and white, 16mm.

Purchase: $75.00 (#51)
Rental: $15.00 (#51)

Sound: Harold Seletski

ASK ME, DON'T TELL ME

American Friends Service Committee
1960

22 minutes, black and white, 16mm.

Purchase: $95.00 (#17)
Rental: $5.00 (#10, #17, #27, #36, #42, #61)

Director: David Meyers

Awards

Golden Gate Award, San Francisco International Film Festival

THAT'S ME

Americans have a remarkable habit of patronizing foreign people, most of the time without realizing it. *That's Me* uncovers this phenomenon in a Spanish situation. A social worker approaches Juan Doya strumming peacefully on his guitar in Central Park, New York City, and begins a conversation.

Social Worker: Not doing anything?
Juan: I'm playing the guitar. O.K.? Yeah, doing nothing, missing school.
Social Worker: Why not go to school?
Juan: The teachers talk too fast. They have a language problem.
Social Worker: Well, why not change schools?
Juan: I been to three.
Social Worker: I mean change to a technical school.
Juan: Ha! And hurt my fingers? My guitar. Or be a secretary? For ladies.
Social Worker: Well, do you want to be like those kids on your block doing nothing but running over rooftops?
Juan: What! Are you crazy? Want to break glass and jump on rooftops? I don't do that. You could get killed.
Social Worker: Ever think of going back to San Juan? You know the people there, the language.
Juan: One, I was never in San Juan. Two, I would like to go back, but all my family and friends are in New York. Three, I don't know anybody there.
Social Worker: Juan, wouldn't you like to earn enough money to buy a car?
Juan: I tell you how to buy a car. First insurance and stinkin' license plates. Then car—used car— then come the parking tickets and repairs.

Social Worker: **A house?**

Juan: **And leave the mortgage for my grandchildren?**

Social Worker: **Wouldn't you like to get married?**

Juan: **No. I just want to play my guitar. Hey! Do you have a car?**

Social Worker: **Well, no. I find it easier to ride the bus.**

Juan: **You have a house?**

Social Worker: **I have an apartment now. Someday a house.**

Juan: **Wife?**

Social Worker: **No. I hope to be married someday.**

Juan: **Ah, you have a girlfriend, eh?**

Social Worker: **Well, no. Not steady. Girls cost money.**

Juan: **You know something?** *I could teach you* **a couple of things.**

That's Me **concludes with a new relationship established between the social worker and Juan. Juan agrees to teach the social worker Spanish and introduce him to some of his girlfriends, and the social worker agrees to teach Juan English.**

The social worker remarks: "You're not doing anything," to which Juan responds "Playing my guitar." "I mean other than that, you're not doing anything." Is there anything wrong with not doing anything in the social worker's sense? What? How does Juan feel about doing something?

"You haven't got anything I want. You're ten years older than I am. If you don't have them, when will I get them?" What does Juan mean? What do you think Juan wants out of life?

Discuss the goals and role of the social worker.

"The teachers are wrong, not me." Is Juan correct? How do you think Juan feels? Does he communicate his feelings to the social worker?

What are the sources of the communication problem between Juan and the social worker?

Act out Juan's dialog with the social worker. Let your conversation express how you would feel as Juan and as the social worker.

ONE MAN'S AUTOBIOGRAPHY

I am a black Puerto Rican. My memories of my childhood in Puerto Rico are of being naked, dirty, hungry and sick most of the time. I had no time for childhood. I mixed concrete, picked fruit, helped build houses. My father came to New York to be with my stepmother, who had left my brother and me and taken her own children. Later he sent for us. Fifteen of us lived in a cellar in the Bronx. At the age of 14 I was a student, a janitor, and an employee in a toilet seat factory. In school we were taught that this country was a great country, that everyone was equal. Yet it was not so. In school I was made fun of because of my color and because I did not speak the language. I could never visit any of my friends'(?) homes. When they had a party, I was excluded. On the street, people looked at us in a strange and funny way. We were always afraid of the white man's reaction to us. This angered me. We were supposedly as good as anyone in this country. The churches were filled with hypocrites who told us to pray and have patience, that it was not their job to become involved in civil rights. I was shipped to Korea in the Army, and there I made

Scene from *That's Me*

up my mind that I would fight whites, my own people and blacks alike for the liberty of all people living in this great country. I will knock down anyone, anything, for this cause. I will put my life on the block. I would rather go to hell than stand by and do nothing, and anyone who speaks evil against any race in front of me will hear from me, a human being, a Christian, a Puerto Rican, a black man, who is sick of hearing: "What can we do; that's how this world is."—The hell it is!

Hector R.

THAT'S ME

Walker Stuart
1963

15 minutes, black and white, 16mm./32mm.

Purchase: $150.00 (#17); in Canada (#74)
Rental: $15.00 (#17, #27)

Producer and Director: Walker Stuart
Photography: Albert Maysles
Sound: David Maysles

Awards

Academy Award Nominee, Best Live Action Short Subject, 1964
Golden Eagle Award, Cine, 1965

INSCAPE

"Inscape" is a term invented by the Jesuit poet Gerard Manley Hopkins to explain the inwardness of things. To him, the most profound inwardness of an individual and the ultimate reality behind all inscape is God.

The film *Inscape* attempts to define this ultimate reality through the eyes of Peter and Ellen, an adolescent boy and girl, who are concerned about self-identity and God. They talk with wild imagination and spend an afternoon of zany argument and hallucination on a beautiful summer beach. Although *Inscape* is a discussion film, superlative camera work and editing techniques clearly derivitive of the best new-wave cinema rank it among the few dialog films for teenagers that succeed.

Why does Peter want to see a "dancing nun"?

His parents want Peter to be like them. What is good about this parental attitude? How does Peter react to this?

From Peter's point of view why does "His walking on the water" have to do with everything?

"This is what we're taught." Does this sound like memorized religion? Is memorized religion helpful for growing Christians? If so, why? Or, why not?

Is he really searching for answers? What are his big questions? What attitude does this searching demand?

Do you believe along with Peter that "the world is in a mess"? "And if the world is something of a mess, so am I!" Does this follow? What are the dimensions of the young-adult "mess"? What can the young generation do about the "world mess"?

"Go in peace. Sin no more." What is this "peace"? What is "sin"?

Scene from *Inscape*

Ellen wants to be herself—to be a woman. She
wants to learn how to tell the world "her thing."
But she does not know her thing. What does it mean
to be a woman in the modern world? Who helps
one become a mature woman? How does one
discover "her thing"?

What is the purpose of it all? Do we need God?
For what?

Evaluate the photography and visual symbolism.

Related material: refer to DISCOVERY IN SONG, Times
They Are A-Changin', page 59

I want to get close to life, feel it and smell it,
sweat over it, and maybe even pick my spot to die.

When I see a guy in a jam, or just needing
somebody's help, I want to be able to leap in, man,
and not stand back and look indifferent while he's
looking anything but indifferent because he's crying
murder or shouting for justice.

I want to be free. Free to laugh, to cry. Free
to die, to live. Free to be responsible, and care,
and dig in. Freedom.

From Free to Live, Free to Die *by Malcolm Boyd.*
Copyright © 1967 by Malcolm Boyd. Reprinted by per-
mission of Holt, Rinehart and Winston, Inc.

I NEED FREEDOM TO BE ME

Who am I in this great big rut? What I want is
freedom.

I'm sick of this same-old-thing jazz and the
laughs that don't make me laugh any more. I'm
tired of doing it because I'm supposed to do it and
anyway what else is there to do? I'm fed up with
the rat-maze and this deep, deep rut in my life.

I need freedom. I need freedom so I can find
out who I am and who these people are I'm swinging
with. . . . I mean, who we really are, underneath
the masks we wear and the roles we play. And I
need freedom to discover the purpose and meaning
of what we're all doing, where we're all heading—
and even if it's where we should be heading.

I need freedom to be me—so I'm not just a
figment of somebody else's imagination or a neat
label on somebody's neatly ordered shelf, but an
actual person who cares and is cared for. I want to
be involved in life, not just an onlooker. I don't
want to watch this ball game; I want to play in it,
hard and all the way.

INSCAPE

National Council of Catholic Men and
St. Francis Production
Los Angeles, California
1968

29 minutes, color, 16mm.

Purchase: $250.00 (#32)
Rental: $15.00 (Spring 1969 N.C.C.M., #32)

Co-Producers: Father Karl Holtsnider, OFM
Richard Walsh
Director of Photography: Bruce Baker
Writer: R. Crean

LINES HORIZONTAL

Norman McLaren is one of Canada's leading
film experimenters. In *Lines Horizontal,* he imposes
a pattern of horizontal lines against a background
of music and color. The horizontal lines progress in

number and motion from simplicity to complexity and return to simplicity; the color scheme parallels this linear development, changing from cool blue to red and finally to blue; Pete Seeger's musical accompaniment follows the same pattern of simplicity-complexity-simplicity.

Lines Horizontal is a visually pleasant film with unusual discussion potential. It has no theme in any traditional sense of the word, yet audiences, if asked seriously enough to uncover a theme, have suggested the widest variety of possibilities. They see in its basic pattern everything from the progression of seasons and the life-cycle to the political dialectic of war and peace. This audience phenomenon is in itself worthy of discussion and pertinent to the fields of psychology and literature. What is the relationship of line, color and sound to human thought and emotion?

LINES HORIZONTAL

International Film Bureau
1963

13 minutes, color, 16mm.

Purchase: $75.00 (#25); in Canada (#77)
Rental: inquire (#25, #36, #42); in Canada (#64, #68, #77)

Created by Norman McLaren and Evelyn Lambert
Music: Pete Seeger

Awards

International Film Festival, Venice, Italy
International Film Festival, Edinburgh

THE DETACHED AMERICANS

The Detached Americans is one of the few badly made films reviewed in this book. The film is included because it has never failed to stimulate discussion.

In a preachy and disjointed manner, *Detached Americans* examines the case of a New York murder. Thirty-eight onlookers watch a man stab a woman to death. The onlookers do nothing to help the woman because they do not want to get involved.

Detached Americans asks the question why and answers it: Americans have created a society of impersonalism in community, career and home. The answer of the film, if accurate, comes across as an indictment, particularly as the constructive comment expressed implies, unfortunately, that former generations were better people. The film seems to ask for cultural regression.

Though most groups are likely to note its cinematic flaws, *Detached Americans* still has the power to provoke lengthy discussion.

Why do the people who witnessed the Genovese murder feel no duty to help?

"Mobility has atomized the family and town." Do you agree? Are there any positive results of mobility in relation to the family and city communities?

Is the background song, Little Boxes, *a valid judgment of new suburbia?*

"Mind your own business. Play it cool. Ask no questions. Keep your mouth shut." How accurate is the film's portrayal of education?

Do you think the personnel manager had a creative

job? How is a working man affected by his job?

Does our American society teach us to spell out and search for personal identity in terms of what we wear and own? If so, why?

Recall the roles of husband and wife. Do you think our society assigns such roles to husband and wife? Is there any relation between our schooling and social mores with the roles of husband and wife?

At the family dinner scene, how do you think the daughter felt during her parents' argument? What effect does this type of experience have on the child? Why does the wife refuse to talk to her husband? What do you think are the causes of such lack of communication between husband and wife?

Act out the family dinner scene.

Related material: refer to DISCOVERY IN SONG, *Little* Boxes, *pages 22–23, and* The Sounds of Silence, *pages 20–21*

THE DETACHED AMERICANS

WCAU-TV, Philadelphia
1966

33 minutes, black and white, 16mm.

Purchase: $145.00 (#12)
Rental: $10.00 (#27, #36, #61); in Canada (#70, #76)

Writer: John Keats
Narrator: Harry Reasoner

HUTTERITES

Hutterites **is a standard but well-made documentary about a separatist community of the same name which at present is flourishing in Canada. The Hutterite community was founded by John Hutter four centuries ago. Each subcommunity numbers one hundred members, and there are fifteen thousand Hutterites in Canada. Their belief is religious and fundamental: without God, man cannot exist; in all things that man does, he must praise God. For the Hutterites, work and religion are bound together. Their schooling is essentially religious and community-oriented. All their work and possessions are shared. They believe that their community is ideal and almost never leave it.**

Hutterites **affords an opportunity to discuss the contemporary fascination with community. What are the essential norms for a separatist community? Is such a way of life appealing? In the light of today's social problems, is it permissible? What do the individuals involved gain from their community living? What does society gain? What are the essential differences between a Christian monk, a hippie and a Hutterite?**

In the Hutterite life what contributes most to forming vital community? What is the most essential community force in the American family? In the American parish? In the American city?

Compare the house and manner of living common to the Hutterites with the typical American family life.

What limitations on community (family, parish and civic) formation are imposed by a separatist way of life?

*The world of changing customs and escalating
knowledge is basically foreign to the Hutterite.
Do you think this is good? How does this affect the
Hutterite community? How do the forces of change
in the American family, in the parish and in the civil
community affect the community?*

*According to the film, it is good for community and
happiness to keep the younger generation at home
and under control (no radio, TV, music). What
good or bad might come of this attitude?*

*"No people concentrate more on the formation of
their children. . . ." Would you agree? Compare
this statement to the American situation of educating
the child.*

*In their growth the Hutterites have united their work
and their worship very closely. Does this
contribute to forming community? In your experience
what is the typical relationship between work and
religion for an American? What do you think
should be the interrelationship between work and
religion?*

*Compare development of community in this film and
in* Detached Americans.

*Plan guidelines of action for a healthy family
community; for a nourishing parish community; for
a strong, positive civic community.*

Monasticism has been a puzzle to the secular world,
but it has generally gained acceptance for its good
influence and depth of purpose. The present Hippie
and Yippie communities, after brief notoriety, have
been dismissed by most people as shallow movements.
Yet the recent renewal of interest in traditional
Christian and Eastern monasticism and the presence
of the Hippie-Yippie phenomenon lead to questions
about our social mood today and about the points
of similarity between two such outwardly different
communities. Both the monastic and Hippie communities reject present society in order to live a
form of life which they believe to be ideal and
indicative of some future way of life. Both communities feel that they justify their presence in
society by showing how this ideal life is to be led
and how happiness has come to them through their
rejection of secular life.

HUTTERITES

National Film Board of Canada
1963

28 minutes, black and white, 16mm.

Purchase: $135.00 (#43); $73.00 in Canada
(#77)
Rental: inquire (#34, #42); in Canada (#64,
#68, #77)

Awards

1964–65
Chris Certificate Award
Religious Category
12th Annual Columbus Film Festival
Columbus, Ohio
1964–65
Blue Ribbon
Doctrinal and Denominational Topics
American Film Festival
New York, New York
1964–65
Honorable Mention
Melbourne Film Festival
Melbourne, Australia

1965–66
Honorable Mention
Festival of Canadian Films
Montreal International Film Festival
Montreal, Canada

DAVID AND HAZEL

David and Hazel have been married for many years. David is a successful executive and a responsible husband, yet he interprets his responsibility to mean that he must never burden Hazel with a discussion of his business affairs. As a result, David and Hazel and their children live with an accepted absence of intrafamily communication. When David's career is threatened, his personal crisis represents a challenge to their family option of silence.

David and Hazel **is an extreme portrayal, yet every family can identify with its problem. The film should precipitate a frank comparison of family communication habits among its viewers.**

What did David think was the proper task of the "man of the family" and of his wife? Why? How did he feel as he lived out this role?

What did Hazel do when David got moody? Were her actions creative of communication?

Evaluate David's reaction to his daughters Ann (her rejected greeting and rejected allowance) and Pam and to his son (their track conversation and science project conversation). What effects do his attitude and actions have on the children and on his wife? How did his wife Hazel react to his treatment of the children? How important is affection expressed by parents to the teenage girl and to the teenage boy? In general do teenage boys and girls have similar relationships with their parents?

Note the connections between David's conversation at the office and his reactions to his family.

How do you think the children feel as they listen to their parents' arguing? What solutions would you offer to the arguments between parents?

David's reaction to their "first" argument is: "It's past now, let's forget it." Did he forget? What do you think of this attitude?

"Maybe you won't have to carry it all by yourself." Did David carry the burden all by himself?

"I won't have to act anymore. It's so hard to keep on acting. . . . I'd like to share this with you, David." Do you think that David will change? Do you feel that Hazel will keep on "acting"?

What was the source of David's problem? What was the source of Hazel's problem? What would you advise David and Hazel to do?

Related material: refer to DISCOVERY IN SONG, *She's Leaving Home, pages 16–17*

PLAIN TALK—
THE BEST MEDICINE
FOR A SHAKY MARRIAGE

Although non-verbal (without words) communication pervades our daily affairs, verbal (with words) communication is the best medicine for a shaky marriage. By that we mean plain talk—the kind of talk that can help husband and wife to understand what each other is feeling. Communi-

Scene from *David and Hazel*

cation in marriage allows *love* to enrich the relationship by permitting each spouse to appreciate the needs of the other and, ideally, to respond to those needs.

Healthy, completely frank talk on subjects that hurt when brought into the open, may seem difficult. In fact for a couple sharing the intimacy of marriage, it may seem almost impossible.

Children, on the other hand, sometimes express feelings with alarming candor. They may say, "I hate you," or "I wish you were dead." The shocked rebukes of their elders force them to conceal their real feelings, both positive and negative. Little by little, experience reinforces these restrictions. Everyone can recall a time in childhood when punishment was the cost of too much "speaking out."

So there are good reasons why most adults keep their real feelings and their more important secrets to themselves. This is the basis for the reluctance of some to visit a marriage counselor. "My troubles are none of his business," they say as they shrug the matter off.

For many, this reticence is a "must." The more you like someone the more difficult it becomes to express how deeply you feel about that person. So, as a young man nears his engagement he may limit himself to pleasantries and compliments. Also, he may put off discussing realistic expectations for marriage with his fiancee. Once they are married, couples try to regain the ability to talk as frankly as they did in childhood. But this time they will do so in a spirit of safety, understanding and love.

Often, we can admit hurt to strangers when we cannot do so to family members or to those with whom we live closely. How many times have you ridden a busy train or plane and had a person you never saw before open up and tell you intimate details of his life? Have you ever done the same thing?

In marriage counseling a man or woman may describe a series of complaints against the spouse. When the counselor asks whether the offending partner knows how the complainer feels, the answer is invariably no. Nor is any explanation given apart from the fear of a lack of understanding. "I just can't bring myself to talk about these things," comes the reply. Neither will tell the other what it is he feels.

One psychologist who looked into this common attitude discovered that bartenders hear more about marital troubles than anybody else. They serve more "patients" than physicians, psychologists, psychiatrists or priests. They are that indispensable third party who will listen to problems, but seldom give advice. Their confidantes do not really want suggestions anymore than they really want to change. The pity of it is that many couples cannot say to each other what they will confide to a neighbor or bridge partner. To change this pattern is not easy but well worth the effort.

Healthy communication calls for honest talk and more than just the ordinary "give and take." It calls for open discussion with those we *love* most, about the things that count most.

When husbands and wives take time to sit down and discuss their mutual problems, good communication exists. Otherwise, problems tend to become skeletons in the closet—off limits for discussion.

From C. and A. Riker, Understanding Marriage *(Deus Paper, 1963), pp. 34–36*

DAVID AND HAZEL

National Film Board of Canada
1963

28 minutes, 3 sec., black and white, 16mm.

Purchase: $165.00 (#28); in Canada $87.00
(#77)
Rental: $8.00 (#17, #36, #61); in Canada
(#64, #68, #77)

A TRUMPET FOR THE COMBO

**Should discrimination in favor of black people
play a part in alleviating the present racial crisis?**
A Trumpet for the Combo **examines this possibility
in the context of a high school. School authorities
favor the selection of a black trumpet player, Bruce,
for a student dance combo, although a white student
is more competent.** *A Trumpet for the Combo*
**reveals the motivation of pro and con within the
high school situation. Since most audiences have
not thought carefully about race relations from this
particular point of view, discussions of the film
usually uncover many hidden racial attitudes.**

*Was it really discrimination to take Bruce on? State
all the arguments pro and con.*

*Should the students listen to the principal or should
they decide for themselves?*

Did the principal have a right to offer his suggestions?

In a similar situation how would you feel *if you were
Bruce? If you were a member of the band? If you
were Mr. McFadden? If you were Bruce's rival?
What would you think and do?*

*Does the filmmaker remain impartial? If not, how
does he betray his own feelings?*

Prejudice is an attitude founded on a pre-judgment
*—a judgment made before enough of the truth is
known. Feeling is often the clue to prejudice or
unreasoned pre-judgment. How do you feel about
people on welfare, about integrated unions and
managements (e.g., building trades or printing
trades), about open housing? What facts do you
know right now about welfare, jobs, housing? Does
your current knowledge of facts warrant your current
feelings? What further facts should you search out
before you are in a position to make a reasoned
judgment?*

EQUAL OPPORTUNITY OR PREFERENTIAL TREATMENT?

"Preferential treatment is not a wholly new
concept on the American scene. In a very real sense
we have witnessed it for decades—for whites. Separate and *unequal* schools, favoritism in hiring and
employment, restrictive housing practices—often
these were preferential treatment based on race.
Universities have admitted less qualified students
who were the sons of alumni, or who played band
instruments at football games between groups of
preferentially treated students. Government
expenditure (and tax) policy has given preference
(some desirable—the War on Poverty; some
undesirable—tax exemption of interest on state and
local bonds). . . . preferential treatment can mean
many different things and can take many different
forms. . . .

"Attitudes to the phrase 'preferential treatment'
can vary with the policy that it calls to mind. Some
may favor compensatory or supplemental educational
programs and relaxed admission standards by
universities, but oppose preferential hiring policies
by private employers. Some may favor programs
to assist the Negro to attain required levels (via

Scene from *A Trumpet for the Combo*

tutorial programs, on-the-job training, retraining, summer educational programs) but oppose preference except through such 'compensatory' programs. Some may feel preference means assistance; others may feel it implies lowering of standards. And persons may disagree on the amount of preference to be granted. If assistance, how much? If relaxation of standards, how far? Does preference mean filling a vacancy with a Negro rather than a white when they are equal in all relevant respects, when the Negro is only a little less qualified, when he is substantially less qualified? Does preference mean extra dollars for Negro schools (how many dollars); does it mean extra training and upgrading programs (if so, how many)?

"Preferential treatment programs can be best discussed and evaluated as specific programs on their individual merits, each with its own costs, each with its own benefits. But all such programs share three things in common: (1) their goal is to speed progress . . . ; (2) they are more readily accepted when they are designed to upgrade and remove disabilities or deficiencies rather than to 'overlook' them; (3) they are more readily accepted when preference for some does not mean retrogression for others."

From R. Fein, "An Economic and Social Profile of the Negro American," in Daedalus, *The Negro American, Fall 1965, pp. 842–843.*

A TRUMPET FOR THE COMBO

National Film Board of Canada
1966

8 minutes, black and white, 16mm.

Purchase: $60.00 (#43); in Canada $33.00 (#77)
Rental: $5.00 (#27, #17); in Canada (#64, #68, #77)

Award

Landers Film Festival
New York, New York

SKY and LEAF

Sky, **also titled** *A Day in Western Canada,* **moves traditionally from morning to evening and from calm sky to stormy weather in a beautiful array of mountains-sunrise-shining-waterdrop photography. Long exposures frequently add a pleasant surrealism to the sky and clouds.**

Leaf **tells the story of an autumn leaf as it blows through Yosemite National Park. Shaken from its tree, the leaf falls over rocks and floats along a stream until it comes to final rest. Like** *Sky, Leaf* **is romantic and beautifully photographed.**

Sky **and** *Leaf* **share a meditative simplicity and have been used to stimulate creative descriptive writing among students. The films, moreover, represent a sharp contrast to much of today's quick-cut, almost pop-art, style of filmmaking and could be shown in conjunction with** *Very Nice, Very Nice* **or** *Science Friction.* **Perhaps the divergent film styles represent different theories of noticing. The audience might find it interesting to analyze the difference and reflect it in their own style of writing or filmmaking.**

How does your *environment contribute to your sense of beauty and life?*

*Are you growing more aware of your environment
—its beauty, its shadows, its process, its limits?*

*Are you becoming aware of its effect on your moods
and values?*

*Are you sensitive to simple beauties surrounding
your daily life? How does one grow in sensitivity to
the beauty of common things?*

*Are you growing more sensitive to persons—
sensitive to the individual qualities of persons?*

Could you see Sky *and* Leaf *as visual parables?
Explain the meaning.*

How does the artist in Leaf *use color, light and
shadow, and movement to bring his subject alive?*

What did you feel as you watched Sky? *Was there a
process or development of your feelings?*

*Trace your moods as you watched these poetic
films. Consider how much your mood may be
dependent on such an environment. How can you
program or educate your moods?*

ASTROMETAPHYSICAL

Lord, I have loved your sky,
Be it said against or for me,
Have loved it clear and high,
Or low and stormy;

Till I have reeled and stumbled
From looking up too much,
And fallen and been humbled
To wear a crutch.

My love for every Heaven
O'er which you, Lord, have lorded,
From number One to Seven
Should be rewarded.

It may not give me hope
That when I am translated
My scalp will in the cope
Be constellated.

But if that seems to tend
To my undue renown,
At least it ought to send
Me up, not down.

From Complete Poems of Robert Frost. *Copyright 1947
by Holt, Rinehart and Winston, Inc. Jonathan Cape Ltd,
Publishers. Reprinted by permission of Holt, Rinehart
and Winston, Inc.*

HURRAHING IN HARVEST

Summer ends now; now, barbarous in beauty,
   the stooks rise
      Around; up above, what wind-walks! what
        lovely behaviour
      Of silk-sack clouds! has wilder, wilful-wavier
Meal-drift moulded ever and melted across skies?

I walk, I lift up, I lift up heart, eyes,
      Down all that glory in the heavens to glean our
        Savior;
      And eyes, heart, what looks, what lips yet
        gave you a
Rapturous love's greeting of realer, of rounder
   replies?

And the azurous hung hills are his world-wielding
   shoulder
      Majestic—as a stallion stalwart,
        very-violet-sweet!—
These things, these things were here and but the
   beholder

Scene from *Leaf*

Wanting; which two when they once meet
The heart rears wings bold and bolder
 And hurls for him, O half hurls earth for him off
  under his feet.

Gerad Manley Hopkins From The Poems of Gerard
Manley Hopkins. *Copyright 1948 by the Oxford University
Press, Inc. (Third edition, 1948), page 74*

SKY

National Film Board of Canada
1961

10 minutes, color, 16mm.

Purchase: $120.00 (#17); $33.00 in Canada
 (#77)
Rental: $6.00 (#17, #34); in Canada (#64,
 #68, #77)

Producer: Robert Edmonds

LEAF

Pyramid Film Production
1962

7 minutes, color, 16mm.

Purchase: $85.00
Rental: inquire (#41);

Producer: Fred Hudson
Music: Fred Katz

TWO MEN AND A WARDROBE

Knife in the Water **has established Roman
Polanski as an important contemporary filmmaker.**
Two Men and a Wardrobe **represents an early and
enjoyable Polanski, full of Polish humor while being
serious and intensely symbolic.**

 **Because of its allegorical nature, the story line
in** *Two Men and a Wardrobe* **is particularly
important. Two men emerge from the sea carrying
a large wardrobe. They walk to the nearest city and
encounter a series of rejections because of their
wardrobe. Their journey partakes of the Everyman
style of allegory, each incident confronting the
viewer with a different aspect of human weakness.
At the conclusion of the film, the two men, still
carrying their wardrobe, walk back into the sea.**

 To make an exacting analysis of *Two Men and
a Wardrobe,* **the audience ought to recall the film
sequence by sequence, fill in cinematic and symbolic
details, and relate them to the meaning of the film.
A mimeographed work sheet with tentative sequence
titles, such as the one printed below, could be
prepared for the audience.**

CREDITS AND OPENING
*The film opens with traditional symbolism. What
expectations do these images establish in the viewer?
Note that Polanski indicates the time of day by use
of shadows at the start and conclusion of the film.*

BEACH SEQUENCE
*The frolic and dance elements in this sequence are
very evocative. Is Polanski trying to communicate a
sense of birth, evolution, sexuality, or simply a sense
of early morning rising?*
*How does the wardrobe mirror function in the
sequence?*

Scene from *Two Men and a Wardrobe*

TROLLEY SEQUENCE

How does Polanski achieve a mood of rejection at the trolley car in terms of camera angle and type of shot: medium, distant, close-up, etc?
The fate of the men is clearly related to the fate of the wardrobe. Why? Should this be so?

GIRL SEQUENCE

The opening close-up and concluding distance shot give this sequence a remarkable beauty. How does the sequence fit into the total meaning of the film? How does the music vary from sequence to sequence? What difference does that make?

HIGHWAY-THEFT SEQUENCE

This sequence, short with a strange humor in it, is a good change of pace for the relatively long sequences on either side of it.
Note that not all of the incidents in the film happen to the men. Is there any method to the switching back and forth between confrontation and observation?

RESTAURANT SEQUENCE

Polanski once again reveals his sense of humor in this sequence. It would be good to analyze this humor and to point out how it is achieved with camera and sound.
What would be possible life-histories for the different characters dining in the restaurant?

LUNCH SEQUENCE

Polanski is midway in the film and for the moment back to the sea. The sequence opens with a curious shot of a fish which at first appears to be floating in the sky, the shot of it angled upward; it then becomes clear that the fish is actually resting on the wardrobe mirror and that the angle of the shot is downward with the sky reflected in the mirror. The fish itself and the entire meal are obviously allusive. There is also a distant shot which communicates a suspension of time.

HOTEL SEQUENCE

At this point, it might be helpful to enumerate the vices developed from the beginning of the film, including the major one of vanity indicated in this sequence.
Polanski seems preoccupied with the puddle of water in front of the hotel; is it possible to read any method into his use of it?

STADIUM-GIRL-FIGHT SEQUENCE

While noting the function of the broken mirror and the sea in this sequence, it may be a good time to discuss the significance of the wardrobe to the entire film.
The personalities of the two men are also revealed more fully here than ever before.

BRIDGE-DRUNK SEQUENCE

Why, at this point in the film, is the drunk included?

BARREL YARD SEQUENCE

Can this film be interpreted on a homosexual level? The fact that all barrels are round probably has something to do with this sequence.

MURDER SEQUENCE

The two men have been more and more personally attacked during this film. Perhaps this sequence is a warning.

BACK TO SEA SEQUENCE

Why is there a boy making countless sandcakes on the beach at the end of the film?

TWO MEN AND A WARDROBE

Polish Film University
1957

15 minutes, black and white, 16mm.

Purchase: $175.00 (#17); in Canada $180.00
(#68)
Rental: $25.00 (#17, #27, #36); in Canada
16mm. for audience under 100—$7.50; 16mm.
for audience 100 to 499; 35mm. for audience up
to 499—$12.00 (#68)

Director and Editor: Roman Polanski

Awards

Bronze Medal Award, International Festival of
Experimental Films, Brussels, 1958

THE CRITIC

The Critic **is a film about an elderly gentleman
and his local theater. Their conversation runs
something like this:**

Elderly Gentleman: **Now dis is cute. What da
hell is it! Must be a cartoon about birth. Two dollars
for a French movie an' I gotta see dis. Looks like a
bug up there. No—two tings in love. Da sex life of
two tings.**
Local Theater: **WILL YOU SHUT UP!**
Elderly Gentleman: **I'M SEVENTY-ONE.
I GOT A RIGHT TO BE LOUD.**
Local Theater: **SHHHHHHHHH**
Elderly Gentleman: **It must be symbolic.
Symbolic of junk. I don't know much about
psychoanalysis, but I'd say that dis was a dirty
picture!**

**How does an older person react when confronted
with an abstract cartoon? Perhaps like the gentleman
above.** The Critic **is a short cartoon that highlights
the humor and laughter in everyday life. An audience
would gain immeasurably from an exchange of such
stories—humorous life vignettes—in which they
themselves have been involved.**

*What is good, and what is bad, about making comedy
and jokes about sacred things (like God, sex,
country, ethnic heritage, individual human dignity)?*

*What are some different types of humor? Give
examples of situation comedy, puns, national jokes,
horror and moron stories, sex jokes.*

*What is the difference between constructive and
destructive humor? Give examples.*

How does one develop his sense of humor?

*Are Christians overly sensitive to the irreverence
of humor? Do they take themselves too seriously?
Is discussing this film at all an example of this?*

THE CRITIC

Ernest Pintoff
1963

41 minutes, color, 16mm., animated

Purchase: $120.00 (5 yr. lease—#17); in Canada
(#74)
Rental: $7.50 (#8, #16) $15.00 (#17)

Producer and Director: Ernest Pintoff
Created and Narrated by: Mel Brooks

Awards

Academy Award
Golden Eagle Award, Cine, 1963

APPENDIX TO COMMUNICATION

Interview with Bruce Gordon
The Hole
Place in the Sun
A Divided World
Thursday's Children
The World of Three
Roadsigns on a Merry-Go-Round
Merry-Go-Round
No Reason to Stay
Propaganda Films
You're No Good
Happy Birthday, Felisa
Science Friction

*Related material: for readings on Communication
confer DISCOVERY IN WORD (Glen Rock, N.J.: Paulist
Press, 1968), pp. 3–26*

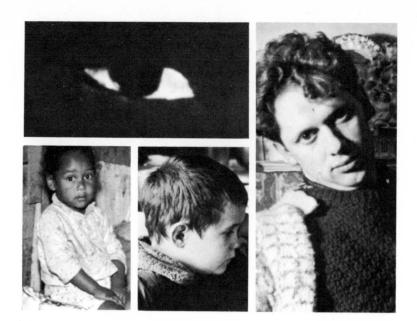

FREEDOM

The Hand
The Bespoke Overcoat
Christmas in Appalachia
Hunger in America
Interview with Bruce Gordon
Black and White in South Africa
Harlem Wednesday
No Reason To Stay
Ginsberg and Ferlinghetti
The Days of Dylan Thomas
Henry Moore
LSD: Insight or Insanity?
The Seekers
The World of Three
Thursday's Children
Television Commercials

THE HAND

The Hand is a cartoon allegory presented by Harry Bellafonte. A man in a room, apparently isolated in the universe and suspended in outer space, cares for his plant and attempts to fashion a clay flower pot for it. A white-gloved hand interrupts and changes the shape of the clay to that of a hand. The man rejects this change and insists on his flower pot shape. The hand attempts to bribe the man—a hand means so much more than a flower pot. It is a symbol for man the maker, for justice, liberty, power and friendship. But the man insists on his flower pot. The hand places the man in a cage and forces him to chisel a huge hand from stone. The man escapes back to his room. There his flower pot accidentally falls on his head and kills him. A black-gloved hand conducts the funeral arrangements with delicacy and honor. The man has, after all, won his own kind of victory.

What meaning did you see or read into this allegory? What did "the hand," the sculptor and the flower symbolize?

Why did the sculptor receive "the hand" with honor at its first arrival?

What were the various forms of "the hand" as presented, especially on TV?

What was the sculptor's growing reaction to "the hand's" resistance? How does he receive the rewards for sculpturing "the hand"?

Explain how he dies. What role does "the hand" play in his death and wake? Why does the flower finally blossom at his death?

Does the fact that this film was created in Czechoslovakia tempt you to interpret the meaning in a certain manner?

Develop a visual parable concerning your own insight on life.

Related material: refer to DISCOVERY IN SONG, Changes, page 135

PRESSURES FOR FREEDOM OR DETERMINATION

The truth, the central stupendous truth, about developed countries today is that they can have—in anything but the shortest run—the kind and scale of resources they decide to have. . . . It is no longer resources that limit decisions. It is the decision that makes the resources. This is the fundamental revolutionary change—perhaps the most revolutionary mankind has ever known.

U Thant, Secretary General of the UN

In the past, men could shrug their shoulders in the face of most of the evils of life because they were powerless to prevent them. . . . Now there is no one to blame but ourselves. Nothing is any longer inevitable. . . . It is in human power for the first time to achieve a level of human welfare exceeding our wildest imaginings or to commit race suicide, slowly or rapidly. The choice rests only with us.

Jerome Frank, "Galloping Technology; A New Social Disease"
Above 2 quotes are from The Dynamics of Change, *Don Fabun, Prentice-Hall, Inc., Englewood Cliffs, N.J.*

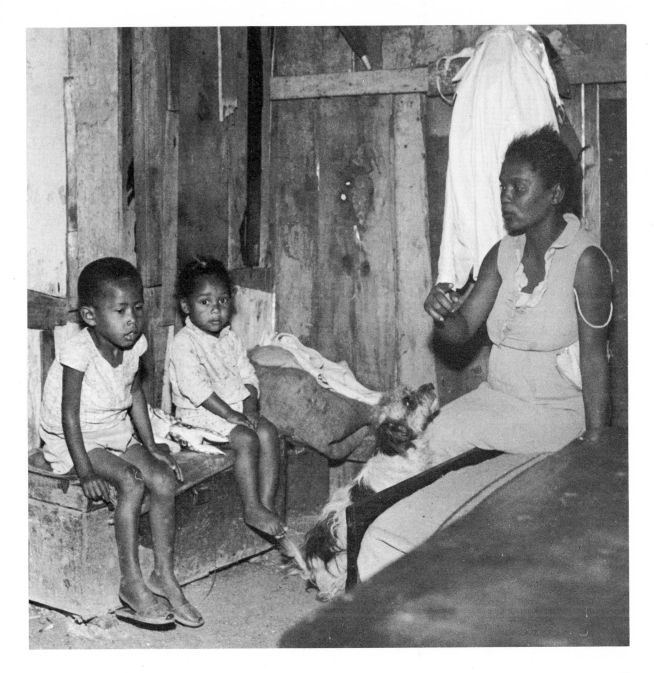

"Do I dare disturb the universe?"

"Love-Song of J. Alfred Prufrock", T. S. Eliot

On the morning, the first morning, of the fall term, a cluster of whites armed with axe handles, lead pipes and chains pounced on the 159 Negro youngsters who showed up, lashing out at boys and girls alike. By noon, the rabble outside had grown to 400. Cheered by their womenfolk, Grenada's vigilantes savagely attacked terrified Negro children as they emerged from school. They trampled Richard Sigh, 12, in the dust, breaking a leg. Another twelve-year-old ran a block-long gauntlet of flailing whites, emerged with bleeding face and torn clothes. Still other Negro youngsters were thrown on the ground and kicked. "That'll teach you, nigger!" "Don't come back tomorrow."

Time, *Sept. 23, 1966*

"I hear America singing, the varied carols I hear"

Walt Whitman

"I earn my living.
I make enough to get by
and it takes all my time.
If I had more time
I could do more for myself
and maybe for others."

Carl Sandburg from The People Will Live On

You shall know the truth, and the truth shall make you free.

THE LITTLE PRINCE

. . . He went back to meet the fox.

"Goodbye," he said.

"Goodbye," said the fox. "And now here is my secret, a very simple secret: It is only with the heart that one can see rightly; what is essential is invisible to the eye."

"What is essential is invisible to the eye," the little prince repeated, so that he would be sure to remember.

"It is the time you have wasted for your rose that makes your rose so important."

"It is the time I have wasted for my rose—" said the little prince, so that he would be sure to remember.

"Men have forgotten this truth," said the fox. "But you must not forget it. You become responsible, forever, for what you have tamed. You are responsible for your rose . . ."

"I am responsible for my rose," the little prince repeated, so that he would be sure to remember.

From The Little Prince, Exupéry, *Harcourt, Brace and World*

THE HAND

Jiri Trnka
1965

19 minutes, color, 16mm.

Purchase: $225.00 (#17); in Canada (#74)
Rental: $25.00 (#17)

Presented by Harry Belafonte
Designed and Directed by Jiri Trnka
Photographed by Jiri Safar
Original Music by Vaslav Trojan

THE BESPOKE OVERCOAT

Nikolai Vasilyevich Gogol has been compared to Charles Dickens for his insight into Russian society through satire and character portraiture. Gogol recorded in his stories an unforgettable picture of Russian society and expressed deep compassion for

the miseries endured by the common people because of social inequity. Gogol had an eye for the suffering peasant character whose sense of humor and wisdom endowed him with a human spirit superior to the bureaucracy of power and wealth.

The Bespoke Overcoat is an excellent film rendition of one of Gogol's most famous stories. Extreme light-shadow contrast and perfectly composed medium-close-up shots create a moody heaviness which captures Gogol's empathy for the poor. The story itself is simple. Maury, a tailor, is visited by his recently deceased friend, Fender. Before Fender can rest in peace, he must have retribution from his former employer, the manager of a clothing warehouse. His employer had paid little money or attention to Fender during his long working life and finally fired him, without pension, because of old age. Maury had been kind enough to make Fender a new overcoat, bespoke, or contracted, for very little money. Fender, returning after death, asks Maury's help again. Both Maury and Fender go to the clothing warehouse and take an expensive overcoat in symbolic retribution. Fender then returns to the underworld. It is implied that the entire story is a reflective daydream of Maury.

The Bespoke Overcoat has a pervasive dry peasant humor, but the last lingering frame of the film, an empty graveyard cart rattling along the cobblestone street, speaks volumes of desolation and emptiness. Somehow *The Bespoke Overcoat* contains within it centuries of Old World suffering and wisdom and patience. Fender summarizes generations of thought when he states to Maury: "I dreamed of a flying overcoat, and in its pockets were bowls of soup."

How did Maury feel about Fender, about the young merchant, about wine and dancing, about death?

How do you think Fender felt in his poverty? Contrast his attitude with the young clerk's. Which is better: to be able to share lunch crumbs with a friendly mouse or to be able to walk into the store and command that no mice be there?

What values do Maury, Fender and the merchant express as important in their lives? Relate these to people you see every day.

As the film ends, an empty graveyard cart is seen through the bars of an iron fence. How do you feel about death? What do you think about death? How do your ideas and feelings about death relate to those presented by this film?

What do you think the title means?

Related material: refer to DISCOVERY IN SONG, Now That the Buffalo's Gone, *page 53*

DEATH

A dying person has nothing better to leave to those around him than signs of his love and signs of his hope. And proofs of love and hope are also the last things that family and friends can provide for a dying man. Sometimes they can express these things in words; at other times merely through their faithful presence. As the hour of death approaches, the household can say parts of the "prayers for the dying." They can call a priest to say these prayers along with them. When the dying person has expired, the last part of these prayers are said: "Come, you holy ones of God, you angels of the Lord, come to meet him. Take him and bring him before the Most High." With this hopeful wish Christians take leave of their dead. The earthly man whom we have known and loved no longer moves, speaks or exists. The limbs remain sound for a while, but it is an outward form that is empty within. Man returns to the earth like an autumn leaf or an animal. It is an intolerable mystery, which man cannot fathom. Death is not in man's nature.

Death is radical. It is not that just the arms, legs, trunk and head die. The whole earthly man dies. Here the deniers of immortality are right. Death is the end of the whole man as we have known him.—Our hearts bid us be reverent in the face of death. Silence falls. Even the Marxist who should believe that the spirit is only a by-product of the body-cells, does not hurry away the dead, but pays them honour. The human heart is filled with awe before this dark gate, as before a mystery. This is the profound intuition of mankind as a whole.

The Scriptures and the Power of God

As we begin now to proclaim the good news which Christ gave about this mystery, we put a very human question. Does nothing of man really remain? Has the dead person utterly disappeared? Is the love and insight of a human life suddenly extinguished at death?—No; the warmth and light which someone has spread continue to live in others. It is marvellous how strong a person's influence can remain after death. Most creative of all is the effectiveness of a good life. And this continues in mankind even when the memory of the name and person has completely vanished. The good done by someone long ago to a child's grandmother can still be one of the factors moulding the child's life. The insights and affection of thousands long dead live on in the present day. The dead are still among us.

But surely not in person?—But perhaps they live on in this way more personally than we often imagine. After all what is more a man's own than the warmth of his love and the light of his wisdom?

This is uniquely verified in the life of Jesus of Nazareth. Since he died and was buried, his spirit has never ceased to be active. On the contrary, he still stirs men's conscience and renews their lives by his love, his words and his power. He has a deeper influence on more men than any who are alive today. It seems as though his death does not matter. While our own great-great-grandfathers are often hardly even names to us, Christ remains a real person. It may still be said that no matter how "personal" the influence of one who is dead and gone, it is still not the man himself. Surely the self, the person, has disappeared? Let us first consider Christ once more. He is not merely recalled and admired from afar, like Rembrandt or Madame Curie. He is spoken to and loved. When we remember him in our liturgy, he is among us. We recognize that he lives, and lives in the truest sense of the word. His influence on mankind is so deep and marvellous precisely because he *himself* is present through his Spirit. He is with us, to exhort, strengthen, and console.

This faith in the resurrection of Jesus is the heart of the gospel which is proclaimed in this book. No one who believes in the good tidings can say that no one has ever come back from the dead. We believe that the Lord showed himself after his death. In the midst of this mystery of dissolution which is death, God has appeared. This is the foundation on which our hope is built: life is stronger than death. And this is true not only of Christ, the first-born from the dead, but for all those whom he knows as his own. They shall follow him. Man is not made to vanish like the beasts.

From A New Catechism (*Herder and Herder*), *pp. 470–472*

THE BESPOKE OVERCOAT

Go Pictures

33½ minutes, black and white, 16mm.

Purchase: $235.00 (#18)
Rental: inquire (#61); in Canada $10.00 (#73)

Based on a short story by Nikolai Gogol
Adapted by Wolf Monowitz
Producer: George K. Arthur

Award

Academy Award

CHRISTMAS IN APPALACHIA

Christmas in Appalachia **portrays American poverty in the Kentucky mountains at one of its most difficult times: winter, December and Christmas. Norman Howe does not go to school because, as the camera shows, he has no adequate clothes; Janet Baker does go to school because the government lunch there will be her only hot meal that day. School is a one-room building with a central stove and companionship. Home is a struggle to make welfare rations stretch and an attempt to bake Christmas biscuits out of government ingredients; for I. B. Johnson, it is a waiting place for the job-training he requested a year ago; and for the Johnson children, five of them, it is a place where Santa Claus, for this year at least, cannot come.**

In this manner, Charles Kuralt, in a CBS News special report, pieces together the story of Appalachian poverty. Cinematically, *Christmas in Appalachia* is superior to average television. The camera adds sympathy to its news-style realism, and the result is a quiet photographic passion. The film is particularly suitable for Christmas showings and can easily be related to a general study of poverty.[1] In one New York high school, the film prompted a yearly summer program staffed by the students in Appalachia.

What did you see in the faces of the people of Appalachia—Mrs. Baker, Janet, Mr. Howe and Norman, I. B. Johnson and his family, Calvin Johnson and his wife Goldie?

How does poverty affect the spirit of the adults? the teenagers?

Compare the homes, the clothes, the facilities you saw in the film with your own. How do your clothes, your home, the conveniences of your life affect your attitude toward yourself and the world?

The mean yearly salary for a family of four in one of the Appalachian counties is $1,500. What is the mean salary in the United States? How many poor persons live in the United States? (The norm for poverty is $3,000 for a family of four, $1,500 for a single person.)

Does the film suggest directly or indirectly who is at fault in this situation of Appalachian poverty? Who should contribute to correcting this destructive situation? What remedies would you offer?

How did you feel as you shared very remotely the poverty experience of the Appalachian residents? What could you do to help alleviate their situation?

[1] *For example, see* The Other America *by Michael Harrington* (Penguin Paperback: New York, 1964).

Scene from *Christmas in Appalachia*

CHRISTMAS IN APPALACHIA

Columbia Broadcasting System, Inc.
51 West 52nd Street
New York, N.Y. 10019

Carousel Films, Inc.
1501 Broadway
New York, N.Y. 10036

1964

29 minutes, black and white, 16mm.

Purchase: $135.00 (#12)
Rental: $10.00 (#61, #38, #36, #27)

Producer: Bernard Brinbaum
Narrator: Charles Kuralt

Awards

American Film Festival Blue Ribbon Award—1965
(Social Documentary)

HUNGER IN AMERICA

About 30 million out of 200 million Americans live in poverty. Roughly 10 million out of the 30 million who live in poverty are hungry. *Hunger in America* is a CBS News special report which examines four poverty areas in the United States: the Mexican population in San Antonio, Texas; the tenant farmer families in Louden County, Virginia; the Navajo Indians in the deserts of Arizona; and the Negroes of Alabama.

Some government officials criticized CBS for stating only a single negative viewpoint. Thousands of viewers, however, found *Hunger in America* to be one of the most startling presentations ever made on television and have since written to Congress demanding that immediate measures be taken to alleviate the conditions of the hungry in the United States. *Hunger in America* researches the living rooms and the hospital wards of the poor; it also records the opinions of doctors and social workers. Its conclusion is shocking. No matter what positive efforts have been made on the part of government or individuals, slow starvation has become a way of life for an impressive segment of our population. Whether this manifests itself in brain damage due to malnutrition or in the death of year-old infants weighing less than five pounds, CBS points out that there is in America a human erosion, framed by the hopelessness of the always hungry and the prosperity of the affluent, which seems incompatible with the basic freedom guaranteed to every American. *Hunger in America* has been shown in Congress; one senator commented that it ought to be shown in every classroom.

What did you see in the children's faces and eyes?

A mother of six children had no food in the house and no hope of getting any. How did she answer the reporter's question: "What do you tell your children?" What would you tell your children in such a situation?

What effect does hunger and malnutrition have on learning and education? What other effects does a diet of poor quality food have on a person?

Do you agree with the views of the mayor of San Antonio concerning the children's hunger?

A young man expresses his opinion about anyone receiving handouts, saying "That's a bum!" Do you agree? Why? Or, why not?

Who is responsible for the poverty of the Navajo Indians?

What effect has mechanization of farming had on cotton farmers? Why do the owner-farmers prevent the tenant farmer from raising some crops—e.g., corn?

How many Americans do not know where their next meal is coming from?

What do you think about the food stamp program? Who should run it? Why?

What effects did the CBS report have on the American government? On the American people?

ARMY OF UNITED STATES POOR

In 1947, the bottom 20 percent of American families received only 5 percent of our nation's aggregate income; the top 20 percent received 43 percent; the top 5 percent of families received 18 percent of the income.

In 1965, the last year for which these figures are available, the bottom 20 percent of American families was still receiving only 5 percent of the aggregate income; the top 20 percent's portion was down two points to 41 percent; and the top 5 percent of American families was receiving 15 percent of aggregate income.

In dollar terms, nearly 20 percent of our nation's families had an income of less than $3,000 in 1965; a full 33 percent of our families earned less than $5,000 that year.

Contrary to popular belief, more than 70 percent of our tax money goes to pay for past, present and future wars, while less than 10 percent goes for health, labor and welfare . . . and fewer than 7 percent of the people on welfare rolls are able-bodied males of working age.

WHO ARE THE POOR IN THE UNITED STATES?

I. 9.3 million families in the U.S. in 1963 had incomes of less than $3,000 for the year.

These 9.3 million families amounted to more than 30 million people.

5.4 million of these families (over 17 million people) had yearly incomes of less than $2,000.

Of these 30 million poor, 11 million are children. One third of all poor people in the U.S. are children under 18 years of age—i.e., one out of every five children in the U.S. is poor.

Over 1 million of the children were growing up in families with six or more children, and with annual incomes of less than $3,000.

These 11 million children of poverty are growing up in homes and communities where education, ambition and hope are as scarce as money.

II. 8 million Negroes, nearly ½ of the total Negro population, live in families with less than a $3,000 annual income.

Many of the 4.5 million Spanish-speaking Americans face poverty because of prejudice, inadequate education and language barriers.

III. 6.8 million heads of families are over 65. Half of these families had incomes of less than $3,000 in 1962 and half again of these had less than $1,000 a year.

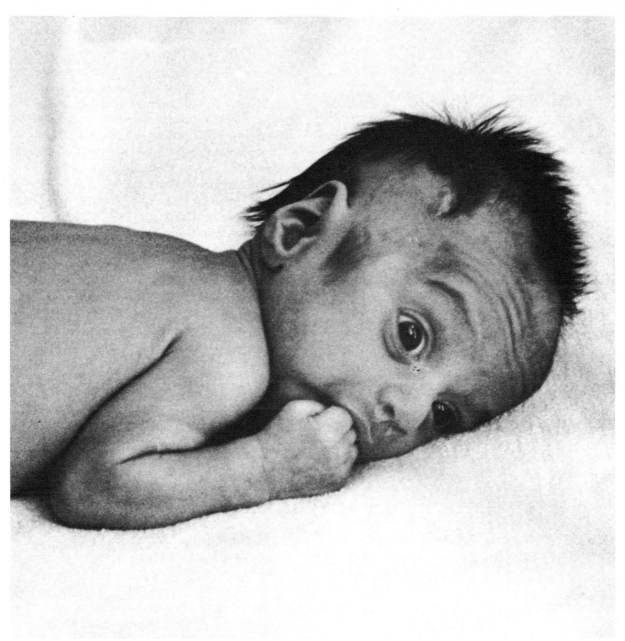

Scene from *Hunger in America*

1.5 million farm families live on less than $250 a month.

WHY ARE SO MANY AMERICANS POOR?

One major cause is lack of education. 61% of families under the $3,000 annual income level were headed by persons who had gone no further than elementary school.

Racial discrimination is a second root of poverty. 45% of non-white families had incomes less than $3,000 a year. A non-white family is 2.5 times as likely to be poor as a white family in our nation.

"We will not win our war against poverty," President Johnson said, "until the conscience of an entire nation is aroused." But this is just the problem—how to arouse the conscience of a fabulously rich nation about the poor?

Christ and the Christian together identify themselves completely with every man in his need. "Truly, I say to you, as you did it to one of the least of these my brethren, you did it to me."

[Consult *The Other America* by Michael Harrington (Penguin) and *In the Midst of Plenty: The Poor in America* by Ben H. Bagdikian (Beacon) to understand the causes and factors of poverty in the U.S.]

HUNGER IN AMERICA

Columbia Broadcasting System Inc.
1968

54 minutes, color or black and white, 16mm.

Purchase: $550.00 color $275.00 black and white (#12)
Rental: inquire (#12)

INTERVIEW WITH BRUCE GORDON

In 1963, Bruce Gordon held the position of field secretary for the Student Non-Violent Coordinating Committee in Selma, Alabama. *Interview with Bruce Gordon* is an uninterrupted monolog. Gordon straddles a chair and talks with sustained inspiration about God and his relation to him, people and love, the racial history of the United States, and the fears of white and black people today. He speaks with depth and beauty.

Interview with Bruce Gordon is one of the most appealing films recommended in this book. Its jiggling hand-held camera and zoom lens technique combine with a rare feeling for expressive close-up shots to suggest a primitive realism and intimacy. *Interview with Bruce Gordon* is an image-breaker for those who have a stereotype picture of black people. In fact, because most audiences respond to the film with deep emotion, it can be discussed by a simple revelation of personal reactions to Bruce Gordon.

Why did Bruce Gordon accept his job as field secretary?

How did he respond to being called "Nigger"? What effect did his army career have on him?

What do you think about his remark: "Self-seekers seldom find themselves"?

Bruce finds evidence of God in modern experience. Would your experience agree?

Are we guilty, as Gordon says? Do we have to pay?

What is Bruce Gordon's own non-violent philosophy? Do you think it is workable?

How much are our racial attitudes formed by our environments?

Who pushes the racial tensions toward violence?

What would Bruce Gordon's reaction be to the problem presented in the film A Trumpet for the Combo?

If you are white, do you have any colored people as friends; if you are black, do you have any white people as friends? Do you think that this degree of racial exchange is necessary before any solution to our racial problems can be successful?

BLACK MEN FEEL

The smells inside the tenement—number 18, 342 East 100th Street, Manhattan—were somewhat more ambiguous. They were a suffocating mixture of rotting food, rancid mattresses, dead rodents, dirt, and the stale odors of human life.

This was to be home. It had been home before: for a family of eight—five kids, three adults. Some of their belongings had been left behind. Some of their life had too.

The place, altogether, was about 25 x 12 feet, with a wall separating the kitchen section from the rest. In the kitchen was a bathtub, a tiny, rusty sink, a refrigerator that didn't work, and an ancient gas range. In one corner was a toilet bowl without a seat. Water dripped perpetually from the box above the bowl. The other room was filled with beds: two double-decker military cots, and a big, ugly convertible sofa. There wasn't room for anything else. The walls and ceilings were mostly holes and patches and peeling paint, sheltering legions of cockroaches.

This was to be my home.

I wondered, for a moment, why.

Then I remembered that this is the sort of place in which most people live, in most of the world for most of the time. This or something worse.

Then I was home.

From My People Is the Enemy *by William Stringfellow. Copyright © 1964 by William Stringfellow. Reprinted by permission of Holt, Rinehart and Winston, Inc.*

God is black. All black men belong to Islam; they have been chosen. And Islam shall rule the world. The dream, the sentiment, is old; only the color is new. And it is this dream, this sweet possibility, that thousands of oppressed black men and women in this country now carry away with them after the Muslim minister has spoken, through the dark, noisome ghetto streets into the hovels where so many have perished. The white God has not delivered them; perhaps the black God will.

From The Fire Next Time *by James Baldwin*

"I'm not throwing any bricks. I'm not looting any liquor stores. But I understand why my 'brother' does, I don't go along with the radicals. But they are necessary to let people know how we feel. If white people don't want to heed Roy Wilkins and Martin Luther King, if we can't get whites to help, we've got to follow Rap Brown.

"At one time I believed this militant talk was detrimental. Now I believe it's the only thing that will get a reaction. I don't worry about the so-called backlash. When I see our real enemies in Congress scuttling civil rights bills, I feel like joining up in a black backlash."

"I'm Not Throwing Any Bricks" by C. Gerald Fraser. Copyright © 1968 by The New York Times Company. Reprinted by permission

INTERVIEW WITH BRUCE GORDON

Harold Becker

1964

17 minutes, black and white, 16mm.

Purchase: $150.00 (#17); in Canada (#74)
Rental: $10.00 (#17, #36, #42)

BLACK AND WHITE IN SOUTH AFRICA

The system of race relations in the Union of South Africa is known as apartheid, most accurately pronounced, according to American black people, "apart-hate." Although the ideal of apartheid is separate but equal societies for black and white, the vast majority of the population, black, live in educational suppression and economic slavery. Free assembly and protest are against the law. In recent history, more than a quarter of a million arrests have been made for violations against the pass law, a suppressive regulation which requires each black person to carry a government pass with him at all times.

Black and White in South Africa evaluates apartheid and the Union of South Africa with accuracy and at times understatement. Its delineation of South African history is clear, and its study of apartheid is rational and dispassionate. *Black and White in South Africa* fascinates and startles with its theme; therefore its style of traditional documentary is acceptable. For discussion purposes, two novels, *Cry, the Beloved Country* and *Too Late the Phalarope* by Alan Paton, himself a South African, make enlightening supplementary reading.

Compare the living quarters of blacks with the cities of the whites of South Africa. Compare the Afrikaner and the native festival. How do you think the black people feel living in such a society?

What feeling did you experience during the "separate-but-equal" sequence? Do you think the "separate-but-equal" policy is a realistic, correct solution to the race problem? What do you think is the source of the white separatist attitude?

In a serious analysis of the American race crisis, a blue ribbon national commission on civil disorders stated: "This is our basic conclusion: Our nation is moving toward two societies, one black, one white—separate and unequal" (U. S. Riot Commission Report, *Bantam Paperback, p. 1). Do you agree? Is this possible in the United States? Would it be good? Why? Why not?*

The narrator quotes the Bible to explain the attitudes of some who defend their apartheid convictions. What do you think of this? Evaluate the Christian attitude toward apartheid.

What is the history of American Christians in relation to the race issue? Do you think the official attitude of present American faiths—Protestant, Catholic and Jewish—expressing strong acceptance of the "riot report," which condemns white racism as chief cause of growing American apartheid, is shared by the ordinary church-goer?

American finance has invested millions of dollars in the Union of South Africa. Does it become a moral concern when an individual discovers that he is, through investing in certain American banks, actually contributing money to a police state?

APARTHEID STATISTICS	White (Europeans)	Black (Africans)
Income per capita	$1,790	$116
Average wage (mining)	$3,800	$210
Income exempt from tax	$ 840	none
Education expenditure per pupil	$ 300	$ 19
Infant mortality per 1,000 births	29	200 plus
Life expectancy	67–72 years	37–42 years
Percent of population (balance Asian and Colored)	19%	68%
Percent of land reserved	87%	13%
Persons in registered trade unions	344,752	none
Persons convicted of pass offenses since 1948	none	5,000,000

Population (1966): Bantu 68.3%; White 19.3%; Colored 9.4%; Asian 3.0%—18,298,000

From "Prejudice in South Africa," in New vol. 3 No. 1. 1968 insert card in this issue

BLACK AND WHITE IN SOUTH AFRICA

National Film Board of Canada

1959

29 minutes, 20 seconds, black and white or color, 16mm.

Purchase: $100.00, color $360.00 (#17); in Canada $87.00 (#77)
Rental: $8.00 (#10, #28, #36, #42, #34); in Canada (#64, #68, #77)

Written by Edgar McInnis

HARLEM WEDNESDAY

Harlem Wednesday presents a collection of paintings by Gregorio Prestopino. Prestopino's subject is the everyday people and scenes of Harlem. He paints children sleeping, an ice man, a fruit shop, a woman ironing, a bit of night life. He is attracted especially to faces and eyes. Harlem Wednesday in this way reaches closer to the meaning of Harlem life than would be possible in an ordinary documentary.

Did you see people or paintings? Was the artist able to share his feelings with you?

What do the eyes in Harlem Wednesday *say about the people? What are they saying to you?*

What do the scenes say about the atmosphere of Harlem?

Tell the life story of the ironing lady, the child or the ice man.

Which tells a truer story: a documentary or a film like Harlem Wednesday?

How did the music affect the visual presentation?

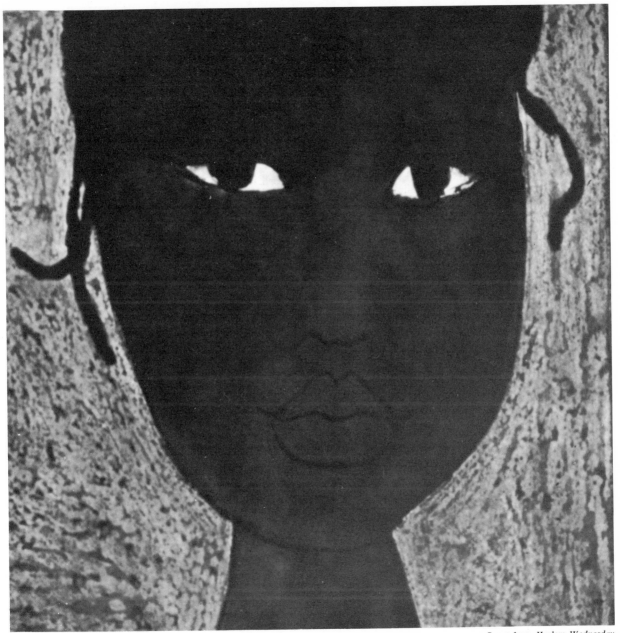

Scene from *Harlem Wednesday*

SEARCHING THE PROMISED LAND

The characters are sons and daughters of former Southern sharecroppers. These were the poorest people of the South, who poured into New York City during the decade following the Great Depression. These migrants were told that unlimited opportunities for prosperity existed in New York and that there was no "color problem" there. They were told that Negroes lived in houses with bathrooms, electricity, running water, and indoor toilets. To them, this was the "promised land" that Mammy had been singing about in the cotton fields for many years.

Going to New York was good-bye to the cotton fields, good-bye to "Massa Charlie," good-bye to the chain gang, and, most of all, good-bye to those sunup-to-sundown working hours. One no longer had to wait to get to heaven to lay his burden down; burdens could be laid down in New York. . . .

It seems that Cousin Willie, in his lying haste, had neglected to tell the folks down home about one of the most important aspects of the promised land: it was a slum ghetto. There was a tremendous difference in the way life was lived up North. There were too many people full of hate and bitterness crowded into a dirty, stinky, uncared-for closet-size section of a great city.

Before the soreness of the cotton fields had left Mama's back, her knees were getting sore from scrubbing "Goldberg's" floor. Nevertheless, she was better off; she had gone from the fire into the frying pan.

The children of these disillusioned colored pioneers inherited the total lot of their parents—the disappointments, the anger. To add to their misery, they had little hope of deliverance. For where does one run to when he's already in the promised land?

From C. Brown, Manchild in the Promised Land (*Signet Book*), *pages vii–viii.*

HARLEM WEDNESDAY

John Hubley

1958

10 minutes, color, 16mm.

Purchase: $120.00 (#17)
Rental: $10.00 (#10, #17)

Award

Silver Lion, Venice Festival

NO REASON TO STAY

Christopher Wood is a high school dropout, and through his eyes No Reason To Stay **takes a hard look at his school system, his parents and his friends. Why was education inaccessible to Christopher Wood? Was there education for him in any part of his school building?**

The boredom of a dull high school lecture and the feverish desire of Christopher to express himself in a world that doesn't want to listen are portrayed with a brilliant style of camera angle and editing. Yet at the conclusion of the film, Christopher's solution is exposed in simple documentary—he rushes from the school building and runs and keeps on running. In No Reason To Stay, **perhaps the fault is everywhere, although audiences seldom think so. As an experiment, teenagers and their parents might be invited to discuss this film together.**

In what way does Chris himself cause his own feelings about school? Do you think he gave the teacher a fair chance to teach or did he just start daydreaming?

"To educate is to interest. To educate is to en-

Scene from *No Reason to Stay*

courage." Is this the most important dimension of education?

Is education "job training"? Is there anything really useful in History, Chemistry, Mathematics, Latin? Is school a "blackmail" for job security?

Is there any reason to stay?

Should Chris have talked to someone else about his ideas on dropping out and education?

How do the adults show concern for Chris' dropping out?

Describe the character of Chris' mother.

Does Chris' girlfriend make the correct decision in rejecting him?

List the significant communication failures in the film. What changes in education would secure more genuine learning experiences?

Why does Chris announce his decision to the whole world?

Compare the film techniques of No Reason To Stay *with* The Game. *How does the director influence the audience?*

INSIGHTS ON TODAY'S LEARNING EXPERIENCE

On Teaching:
"The good teacher must be developed, and above all, encouraged and made aware of his crucial position in the whole educational process. We need teachers who are possessed of the true Catholic attitude of mind which should be soaring, anti-pedantic, open-minded, and filled with respect for reality. We need what someone has called the evocative teacher who brings out responses that are personal and dynamic, and who knows that human growth is experimental, slow but curious, real only if independent, assisted only if encouraged, successful only after floundering. In the last analysis, the system is dependent on the competence, skill, wisdom, prudence, dedication and holiness of the individual teacher. . . . Our young people must learn not to fear a changing world but to shape it in the freedom of the children of God."

Pedro Arrupe, S.J., in "Letter Addressed to Western Catholic Education Association Administrators Conference," in Jesuit Education Quarterly, *Oct. 1967, page 128.*

On Methods:
"The 'tell' em-and-test-'em' process, John Holt claims, not only induces fear and discourages experimentation but leads to a concentration on answers rather than on problems—and it is 'dishonest and the students know it.' Teachers coach the kids for the tests and care more about 'the appearance' of knowledge than real understanding. 'What would happen at Harvard or Yale if a prof gave a surprise test in March on work covered in October? Everyone knows what would happen; that's why they don't do it.' In this 'temple of worship for right answers, the way to get ahead is to lay plenty of them on the altar.' The whole system, insists Holt, convinces most students that 'school is mainly a place where you follow meaningless procedures to get meaningless answers to meaningless questions.' "

From Time, *Sept. 1, 1967, page 37.*

Lawrence Ferlinghetti. Scene from *Ginsberg and Ferlinghetti*

Allen Ginsberg. Scene from *Ginsberg and Ferlinghetti*

On Schools:
". . . in high school, you begin to see an alarming percentage of dull-eyed, defeated kids—even in my high school. What's gone wrong is that the schools have systematically lowered their students' intelligence. They almost literally beat their brains out. And most of the dirty work is done by the teachers.

"Kids are too often rewarded for saying the expected thing and the teacher regards it as a triumph to reduce the best kids to mediocrity. A lot of them are corked-up old hens, and when they see the kids getting on terrain they—the teachers—don't know, their first response is, 'How can I get them back to the stuff I know?' I tell all my teachers to be resourceful, to be opportunistic—a good teacher has to be able to turn on a dime."

"Traffic Jam in the Private Schools" by Richard Schickel. Copyright © 1967 by New York Times, Inc. Reprinted by permission of The Sterling Lord Agency

NO REASON TO STAY

National Film Board of Canada

1966

28 minutes, black and white, 16 mm.

Purchase: $150.00 (#17, #34, #18); in Canada $73.00 (#77)
Rental: $8.00 (#17); in Canada (#64, #68, #77)

Producer: John Kemeny
Director: Mort Ransen
Photography: Mike Lente

Awards

Chris Certificate Award, Columbus Film Festival—1967

Diploma of Merit, Melbourne Film Festival—1967
Slanders Film Award, New York City Film Festival—1966
Blue Ribbon Award, American Film Festival—1966

GINSBERG AND FERLINGHETTI

Who Be Kind To*

**Be kind to your self, it is only one
        and perishable
of many on the planet, thou art that
one that wishes a soft finger tracing the
        line of feeling from nipple to pubes—
one that wishes a tongue to kiss your armpit,
        a lip to kiss your cheek inside your
        whiteness thigh—
Be kind to yourself Harry, because unkindness
        comes when the body explodes
napalm cancer and the deathbed in Vietnam
is a strange place to dream of trees
        leaning over and angry American faces
grinning with sleepwalk terror over your
        last eye—
Be kind to yourself, because the bliss of your own
        kindness will flood the police tomorrow,
because the cow weeps in the field and the
        mouse weeps in the cat hole—
Be kind to your neighbor who weeps
        solid tears on the television sofa,
he has no other home, and hears nothing
        but the hard voice of telephones
Click, buzz, switch channel and the inspired
        melodrama disappears
and he's left alone for the night, he disappears
        in bed—
Be kind to your disappearing mother and
        father gazing out the terrace window
        as milk truck and hearse turn the corner**

Be kind to the politician weeping in the galleries
    of Whitehall, Kremlin, White House
    Louvre and Phoenix City
aged, large nosed, angry, nervously dialing
    the bald voice box connected to
electrodes underground converging thru
    wires vaster than a kitten's eye can see
on the mushroom shaped fear-lobe under
    the ear of sleeping Dr. Einstein . . .

London: June 10, 1965, Allen Ginsberg

* This is the first third of the entire poem which is called "Who To Be Kind To" in the film. Reprinted from a Cranium Broadside (poster), Cranium Press (642 Shrader, San Francisco).

Critics have situated Allen Ginsberg in the Whitman-Sandburg tradition with its pounding, exuberant, chant-like style of poetry. And like Whitman in his day, Ginsberg always appears to poke at the sacred and to shock. He questions our culture's suppression of sensual feeling and challenges the contradiction that our police and military policy sometimes makes with our declarations of independence. Yet if Ginsberg speaks from an "underground" position, he is continually asserting the most traditional of values, the dignity of the individual and human empathy.

The film *Ginsberg and Ferlinghetti* is sympathetic to Allen Ginsberg. He reads several of his poems, one of them "Who Be Kind To," in the various settings of his underground life. The film includes as well something of Ginsberg's life history and poetic theory.

At times Lawrence Ferlinghetti the satirist seems like a schoolboy who has thought of a good joke and revels in the telling of it over and over again to his friends. Yet he is always and pervasively a man of responsibility concerned about the difficulties of the "established" situation. As is also true of Ginsberg, Ferlinghetti possesses a verbal intensity and realist shock imagery, as well as a mounting phraseology that carries its reader naturally into its meaning. Unlike Ginsberg, Ferlinghetti has a more cerebral and deliberate style of poetry and moves more rapidly to general philosophic questions.

The film introduces Ferlinghetti in his position as publisher, owner of City Lights Bookshop in San Francisco, and Doctor of the Sorbonne. The city of San Francisco itself provides background for his reading. The final poem in the film, "Dog," is reprinted here from *A Coney Island of the Mind* (New Directions, 1958) by Lawrence Ferlinghetti.[1]

Lawrence Ferlinghetti, A Coney Island of the Mind: Copyright © 1958 by Lawrence Ferlinghetti. MacGibbon and Kee, publishers. Reprinted by permission of New Directions Publishing Corporation

Discuss the significance of Ginsberg and Ferlinghetti.

What does it mean to be "underground"? In what sense can Ginsberg and Ferlinghetti be said to be "underground poets"?

What is central to the personal value system of "the underground"? How would you evaluate this?

How does the "underground" value system compare with Christian values?

What is its primary quarrel with the "Establishment"? How is this expressed in the poetry of Ginsberg and Ferlinghetti?

Would you like to be a member of the "underground society"? Why? Or, why not?

DOG

The dog trots freely in the street
and sees reality
and the things he sees
are bigger than himself
and the things he sees
are his reality
Drunks in doorways
Moons on trees
The dog trots freely thru the street
and the things he sees
are smaller than himself
Fish on newsprint
Ants in holes
Chickens in Chinatown windows
their heads a block away
The dog trots freely in the street
and the things he smells
smell something like himself
The dog trots freely in the street
past puddles and babies
cats and cigars
poolrooms and policemen
He doesn't hate cops
He merely has no use for them
and he goes past them
and past the dead cows hung up whole
in front of the San Francisco Meat Market
He would rather eat a tender cow
than a tough policeman
though either might do
And he goes past the Romeo Ravioli Factory
and past Coit's Tower
and past Congressman Doyle
He's afraid of Coit's Tower
but he's not afraid of Congressman Doyle
although what he hears is very discouraging
very depressing

very absurd
to a sad young dog like himself
to a serious dog like himself
But he has his own free world to live in
His own fleas to eat
He will not be muzzled
Congressman Doyle is just another
fire hydrant
to him
The dog trots freely in the street
and has his own dog's life to live
and to think about
and to reflect upon
touching and tasting and testing everything
investigating everything
without benefit of perjury
a real realist
with a real tale to tell
and a real tail to tell it with
a real live
            barking
                democratic dog
engaged in real
            free enterprise
with something to say
            about reality
                and how to see it
                    and how to hear it
with his head cocked sideways
            at streetcorners
as if he is just about to have
            his picture taken
                for Victor Records
            listening for
                His Master's Voice
            and looking
                like a living questionmark
            into the
                great gramophone

Scene from *Days of Dylan Thomas*

of puzzling existence
with its wondrous hollow horn
which always seems
just about to spout forth
some Victorious answer
to everything

GINSBERG AND FERLINGHETTI

NET Film Service

1966

30 minutes, black and white, 16mm.

Purchase: $125.00 (#35); in Canada (#68)
Rental: $10.00 (#35, #61); in Canada (#68)

THE DAYS OF DYLAN THOMAS

Do not go gentle into that good night;
Rage, rage against the dying of the light.

The days of the poet Dylan Thomas were noted for their creative energy, much of it squandered in depression and drinking, significant moments of it crystallized into poetry. *The Days of Dylan Thomas* **successfully commemorates the energy and sadness of Dylan Thomas as reflected in his poetry. It combines biographical information, Thomas' reading of his own poetry, for which he was famous, and footage of his native Welsh countryside.**
Dylan Thomas lived for thirty-nine years. He was born in 1914 and died in 1953 after drinking eighteen straight whiskies. He was noted for his humor and wit. His poems frequently celebrate a divine purpose or force within natural process and often he returns to the child's innocent vision of the world.

84

Dylan Thomas represents a paradox and a problem. Is personal tragedy the price of great art? Why is degeneracy and imbalance often associated with art? *The Days of Dylan Thomas* **is a film with good discussion possibilities because Thomas is symptomatic of the life and work of numerous other artists whose problems and options share a universality with at least a passing mood in each of us.**

How did you feel about Dylan Thomas as you watched the picture?

What do you think may have been the cause of his personal tragedy?

Is personal tragedy the price of great art? Do you know of other great artists whose greatness was linked to personal tragedy?

What is the creative artist's responsibility to the community for whom and about whom he writes?

What makes a person creative? Are there different types of creativity? How does one nourish growth in creativity?

Try to write a few lines of poetry expressing a personal experience.

DO NOT GO GENTLE
INTO THAT GOOD NIGHT

Do not go gentle into that good night,
Old age should burn and rave at close of day;
Rage, rage against the dying of the light.

Though wise men at their end know dark is right,
Because their words had forked no lightning they

Do not go gentle into that good night.

Good men, the last wave by, crying how bright
Their frail deeds might have danced in a green bay,
Rage, rage against the dying of the light.

Wild men who caught and sang the sun in flight,
And learn, too late, they grieved it on its way,
Do not go gentle into that good night.

Grave men, near death, who see with blinding sight
Blind eyes could blaze like meteors and be gay,
Rage, rage against the dying of the light.

And you, my father, there on the sad height,
Curse, bless, me now with your fierce tears, I pray.
Do not go gentle into that good night.
Rage, rage against the dying of the light.

THE DAYS OF DYLAN THOMAS

Rollie McKenna

1965

21 minutes, black and white, 16mm.

Purchase: $150.00 (#17); in Canada (#74)
Rental: $15.00 (#17, #36, #42); in Canada
(#64, #78)

Producer: Rollie McKenna
Based on the pictorial biography "The Days of Dylan
Thomas" by Rollie McKenna and Bill Read
Director: Graeme Ferguson

Awards

Golden Eagle Award, Cine, 1966
Grand Prize, Television Film on the Arts, Bergsano,
1965

Diploma of Honor, Locamo Film Festival, 1965
Edinburgh Film Festival, 1965
Cork Film Festival, 1965

HENRY MOORE

**In 1948 Henry Moore received the International
Sculpture Prize in Venice. Moore is noted for his
shaping of space as well as solids and for an intense
psychological comment within his work. He is
generally considered to be the foremost English
sculptor of modern times.**

**The film *Henry Moore* reveals a world seldom
seen by the average person. It studies the method
and art of Moore by examining his work in process
and by asking him questions directly. Moore is well
known for his ability to formulate his philosophy of
life and art, and his comments should stimulate a
good discussion.**

*Would you like to give any of Henry Moore's works
as a gift, say a wedding gift? Would you like to
receive it? Which work would you most like to have?
Which would you least like? Why?*

Does the film suggest to you why *Henry Moore is a
sculptor? Why do you think he is? Couldn't a man as
inventive as this be doing something more
"worthwhile"? Do you consider sculpting worthwhile?
Do you consider looking at sculpture worthwhile?
Why?*

*Can you suggest where in the world—the real world
—Moore got his strange shapes from? Are these
shapes Moore's way of saying something about our
world, or his world? What could he be saying?*

85

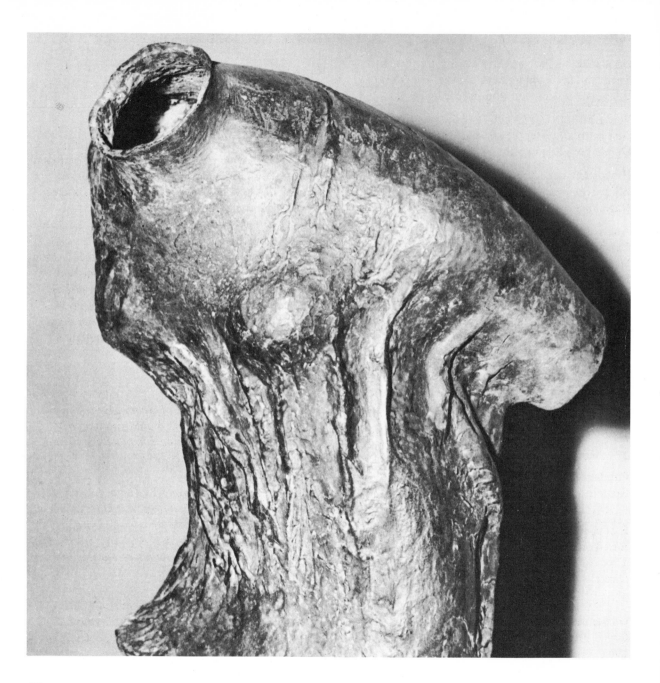

Try to sculpture a piece of wood or plaster of paris into a form expressing your feelings about the world.

What is an artist? Is his creativity an inherited gift or can creativity be nourished and developed? What steps would you say are part of the creative process? What is the function of the artist to the society he lives in?

HENRY MOORE

British Information Service

1952

25 minutes, black and white, 16mm.

Purchase: $135.00 (#17); in Canada (#74)
Rental: $12.00 (#17, #42); in Canada (#68, #78)

LSD: INSIGHT OR INSANITY?

LSD: Insight or Insanity? **takes an informative trip through the tangled world of LSD. Does LSD increase self-knowledge? Does it encourage creativity? How dangerous is it, and what are the odds against its users? In answering these questions,** *LSD: Insight or Insanity?* **combines the traditional style of documentary, a straightforward presentation of information, with an appropriate "psychedelic" style. The camera cuts strangely and colors splash and distort throughout the film's catalog of fact and opinion about LSD.** *LSD: Insight or Insanity?* **is editorially against LSD and is effective. Its editorial position communicates itself strongly, however, and can become a point of challenge during a discussion.** *LSD: Insight or Insanity?* **and any controversy about the validity of its position should open the audience to a candid discussion about drug-related topics.**

How did you feel about the message in the film: Is LSD insight or insanity?

Evaluate some of the motives that a person may have for taking an LSD trip.

What effects may result from an LSD trip?

Act out the role of a counselor who tries to advise a young man not to take an LSD trip because of fear of its results. Compare a reasoned-out approach on the part of the counselor to a fear-and-threat approach.

What alternatives are available to one who wants some extra-special experience (sensate or spiritual) of himself but would like to avoid LSD?

LSD

Q. What is LSD?
A. LSD is a semi-synthetic substance which can alter mental functioning in a profound manner and has been the subject of medical research for several years.
Q. If one takes LSD, what does he experience?
A. Usually, there is a mood change. What one sees, hears and smells is distorted. False beliefs are entertained and the person may see things which are not there. In addition, the user often loses the feeling that he is a cohesive unit. The experience can be pleasant and interesting. Of importance, it can be most unpleasant and even terrifying.
Q. Are there dangers associated with LSD use?
A. Yes, even when taken only once. The user whose mood becomes one of depression may commit suicide. Dominated by false beliefs, he may commit an aggressive act. Impaired judgment may lead to a serious accident. An acute psychotic episode which

Scene from *LSD: Insight or Insanity?*

requires hospitalization may be precipitated. The latter can be prolonged and required extensive treatment. It is feared that some persons who become psychotic may never fully recover.

Q. Assuming the LSD experience turns out to be enjoyable, are there any problems associated with repeated use?

A. Yes. It may cause the taker to drop out of society giving up family, friends and productive activity. Recent studies show that repeated use may cause chromosomal abnormalities which may produce undesirable changes in the user's future children.

Q. If one has emotional problems, can the taking of LSD help?

A. This is presently the subject of medical research. Current information is inconclusive and does not support the contention that LSD facilitates the development of real insight, particularly, when taken in the absence of a trained therapist. The drug has not been authorized for general usage.

Q. Does LSD increase creativity?

A. Despite the claim of users, tests show that LSD does not increase the quality of creative activity. Performance under the influence of LSD only appears to be heightened. The person's perception of performance is distorted while the actual performance level is reduced.

From The Attack, *Feb. 1968, page 2 (published by the New York State Narcotic Control Commission, Albany, N.Y. 12203).*

LSD: INSIGHT OR INSANITY?

Medi-Cine Production

1967

18 minutes, color, 16mm.

Purchase: $200.00 (#5); in Canada $325.00 (28 min.) (#69)

Rental: $20.00 (#5, #27, #61); in Canada (#64, #68, #69)

Producer and Director: Max Miller

THE SEEKERS

"I'm afraid of a lot of things now that I wouldn't have been before."

"I want to make it on my own without drugs."

"It doesn't help you understand yourself."

"All of me was infected."

The Seekers **is a study of drug addiction, marijuana and LSD, and the general theme of adolescent "cop-out," including the hippie phenomenon. This breadth of subject matter is in itself probably a mistake.**

The Seekers **was produced with the cooperation of ex-drug users, all graduates of Day Top Lodge in Staten Island, New York. Much of the film was shot on location and contains the informative and deeply moving statements of the former addicts.** *The Seekers* **is almost sensational in effect and is a successful eye-opener for parents and sympathetic students. This strength, however, is also the film's limitation. Many students find it overemotional and suspect the accuracy of its information.**

At present, within New York State *The Seekers* **is fulfilling an important function. The New York State Narcotic Addiction Control Commission distributes the film and provides lecturers who answer questions and direct the audience discussion. This method of showing** *The Seekers* **is highly recommended.**

Which person in the film impressed you most? Did any of their comments stick in your mind?

"Drugs don't have to be addictive to be dangerous to the person." Would you agree? Why? Or, why not?

One fellow "didn't feel comfortable with people . . . and was scared of people and girls." What would some causes of such fears be? What comfort did he get from drugs?

One girl says that being a hippie is an easy way out, a way of running away, a cop-out. Do you agree? Or, is the world worth adapting to and changing? If the world is all messed up, how can discontent be constructive in changing the scene—our world we live in?

Lynn says it is work, real hard work, to live with another human being, for he has different wants, different needs, and it is hard to express your own feeling, and hard to listen to the other person. How do you feel about this?

Lynn says to her husband (Brendan): "I feel controlled, manipulated in a lot of ways!" Do you know that feeling? Have you ever felt manipulated or controlled?

Brendan says: "I don't ask for what I need." Why? He fears he will lose Lynn because "she is self-sufficient. She can make it without me. I love her and I could lose her." How do you think these fears originate and grow? How would you remedy such fears?

BARBITURATES

Q. What are barbiturates?
A. Barbiturates are useful preparations prescribed in the practice of medicine to induce sleep or quiet an anxious patient.

Q. Can barbiturates be dangerous?
A. Yes. When used to get "high" mental sluggishness, confusion, emotional instability and a lack of coordination result. The more that is taken, the greater these effects. The confusion and lack of coordination lead to accidents. The emotional instability produced can contribute to the performance of aggressive acts. The confused state which results also has caused individuals to lose sight of the number of capsules they have taken. In these instances, overdose—causing coma and sometimes death—has occurred.

Q. Can a person become dependent upon barbiturates?
A. Yes. When taken regularly to promote sleep, the person may become emotionally dependent and find that he is unable to get a normal amount without them. More important, when taken regularly in the excessive doses needed to get "high" both emotional and physical dependence can occur.

Q. What are the consequences of physical dependence on barbiturates?
A. If the person who is physically dependent upon barbiturates should stop taking them abruptly, he feels well at first but then becomes nervous, restless, begins to shake, becomes dizzy, is unable to sleep and may vomit. Convulsions may occur and there is the possibility he will become psychotic. This illness can be severe and some persons experiencing it have died.

"PEP" PILLS

Q. What are "pep" pills?
A. "Pep" pill is a term usually applied to an amphetamine-containing perparation. The latter find use in medicine for the relief of mild depressions and where a suppression of appetite is desirable and indicated.

Q. Is there any danger associated with the use of amphetamines?
A. Yes. While physicians prescribe amphetamines in amounts which are well tolerated, the person who takes them on his own often tends to take too much. As a result the fatigue which is present tends to be masked and tasks are attempted which cannot be handled. This may lead to mishaps. Of importance are the automobile accidents caused by drivers attempting to extend the time they might spend behind the wheel by taking "pep" pills to remain awake.

Q. Are there other problems caused by amphetamines?
A. Yes. Those who take amphetamines on their own in an effort to elevate mood—without seeking help for the difficulties which cause them to feel "down" —often find themselves using the substance on a regular basis. To keep getting the effect of the substance, larger amounts must be taken. Accompanying this ingestion is a growing sense of nervousness. Sleeping becomes difficult. Further, if a large quantity of the drug is taken a psychosis can occur, during which the person entertains false beliefs and hallucinates. Often this psychosis sees the person believing that he is being followed, talked about and persecuted. Such individuals have been known to assault an imagined pursuer.

HEROIN

Q. What are narcotics?
A. The term narcotic drug is applied to a group of preparations which are capable of relieving pain. Morphine, heroin, dilaudid, methadone and demerol are examples of narcotic substances.

Q. Do physicians treat patients with heroin?
A. Heroin has been banned in many western countries because of the ease with which it produces physical and emotional dependence. Consequently, it is no longer prescribed by physicians in the United States.

Q. Where is heroin secured?
A. The manufacture of heroin takes place in clandestine laboratories which are controlled by the leaders of organized crime. They deal through many intermediaries who ultimately make the drug available to the "street pusher" for sale to the heroin user. In the process of changing hands, the original substance is diluted by the addition of talcum powder, quinine and/or sugar. The latter step insures each handler a greater monetary profit.

Q. What are the consequences of physical dependence upon heroin?
A. The individual who is physically dependent upon heroin—within four hours after his last dose—begins to develop an illness which features yawning, perspiration, tearing of the eyes, secretions from the nose and goes on to the development of gooseflesh, muscle twitches, aching bones and muscles, alterations in blood pressure, pulse and respiration, elevated temperature, nausea, vomiting, diarrhea and loss of weight. The peak of this syndrome is reached within 24 to 36 hours.

Q. *Do all users of heroin become physically dependent?*

A. Yes, if the drug is used regularly and in sufficient amounts. Example: a person who uses heroin of good quality regularly for a period of from two to four weeks generally will develop a physical dependence. However, in their quest for profits, pushers are selling such a highly diluted dose that today heroin users develop limited physical dependence.

Q. *Does the regular user of heroin get ahead in society?*

A. Not as a rule. The personality difficulties ordinarily associated with the taking of heroin serves as a substantial obstacle to successful living. These difficulties are further complicated by the need to raise large sums of money, almost always by illegal means, to pay for the drug. Preoccupation with the drug to the exclusion of other interests, such as regular attendance at school and holding a job, adds to the process of alienation.

Q. *How does heroin affect the sex drive?*

A. Most often heroin reduces or even eliminates interest in sexual matters.

Q. *Are narcotic users violent?*

A. The majority of narcotic users are passive people who, when they resort to crime, shy away from violence. The drug itself serves to suppress aggressive tendencies.

Q. *Are heroin users subject to physical disorders?*

A. The heroin user purchases a product from the illicit market which is unsterile and contains many contaminants. Often he injects the substance into a vein using unsterile instruments. As a result, he is subject to abscesses, serious blood infections, tetanus, hepatitis and venereal disease. Since the amount of drug he has bought is unknown, he may take an overdose and die. At times the contaminants are lethal. Regular heroin use tends to be associated with weight loss and poor personal hygiene.

MARIJUANA

Q. *What is marijuana?*

A. In the United States the term marijuana (cannabis) is used to refer to any part of the hemp plant or extract therefrom which can induce physical and psychic changes. The resinous exudate of the top of the female plant contains most of the active ingredients. In the Middle East the resin is called hashish. In the Far East it is called charas . . .

Q. *Are there dangers associated with marijuana use?*

A. Yes. The smoking of a single marijuana cigarette has been known to precipitate a psychotic episode. Heavy use can produce visual distortions, false beliefs and hallucinations. The intellectual and sensory alterations can lead to accidents, aggressive and/or anti-social acts.

Q. *Is marijuana addicting?*

A. Marijuana does not lead to physical dependence. Typically, it is used periodically. Occasionally an individual becomes emotionally dependent upon the drug and seeks its use on a regular basis.

Q. *Is marijuana use increasing in our schools and colleges?*

A. Yes, though most students who use it do so only a few times.

Reprinted by permission, New York State Narcotic Addiction Control Commission

THE SEEKERS

Myron Solin

1968

31 minutes, color, 16mm.

No Rental (#37)

THE WORLD OF THREE

**"She hates me. She stinks. I like her feet."
Lucas is a three-year-old. His relationship to his
mother, his baby sister and the world of objects
around him reflects the complicated perspective of
his age.** *The World of Three* **recreates that perspective with a style of camera angle and editing
that goes beyond the traditional candid shot and is
capable of conveying the looming confusion and
dizzying state of semi-tantrum atmospheric to the
world of a three-year-old.**

**The World of Three deals with the three-year-
old's complete dependence on his mother, his
sibling rivalry and his rage for recognition. Yet by
speaking so eloquently for the three-year-old,** *The
World of Three* **must certainly enlighten the adolescent or adult to his own analogous world. A
discussion with this comparison in mind should
prove interesting.**

*What scene do you think best showed the mother
expressing her love for Lucas?*

*How do you think the boy feels while (a) playing
with his mother with the balloon, (b) building his
blocks, (c) hearing his mother with his little sister,
(d) looking at the tree in the park, (e) testing the
stamp in his father's office, (f) at dinner, (g) going
to bed? How do we experience and grow with similar
experiences?*

*What did the director of the film express by the
distortion of focus when the child was looking at the
vase? When he was looking at his mother? Why did
he muddle the voices on the sound track?*

*Would better communication have changed the
picture—for example, in the vase sequence, the
father's office sequence, the dinner sequence?*

*In what ways are teenagers similar to this three-
year-old?*

*One teenager remarked after seeing this film: "It
wasn't realistic. If I broke a vase, I would have my
tail kicked in. He is a spoiled, typically American
little brat." Would you agree? Why? Or, why not?*

*Why does the director focus on the vase under the
credits of the film?*

LONELINESS AND BECOMING
A PERSON. . . .

The worst thing that can happen to a person is to feel
lonely—really cut off from other people. To feel
that no one wants you, no one cares about you, no
one even recognizes you—this is the worst kind of
suffering, and it leads, often enough, to madness or
suicide.

We need other people in order to discover ourselves.
There is no other way. At the party I began with,
your feeling of being known made you suddenly feel
really yourself, whereas before you were oppressed by
the sense of not being quite "real." You were
paralyzed by a helpless feeling of not mattering, of
not really *being,* simply because you didn't exist as
a person for those other people. They saw the
outside of you, but they didn't care; they didn't *know*
you.

Experiments have shown that a man plunged into
solitude, darkness and silence (even if he volunteers
to undergo it) soon loses his sense of time, of the
reality of things; he loses the desire to eat, the

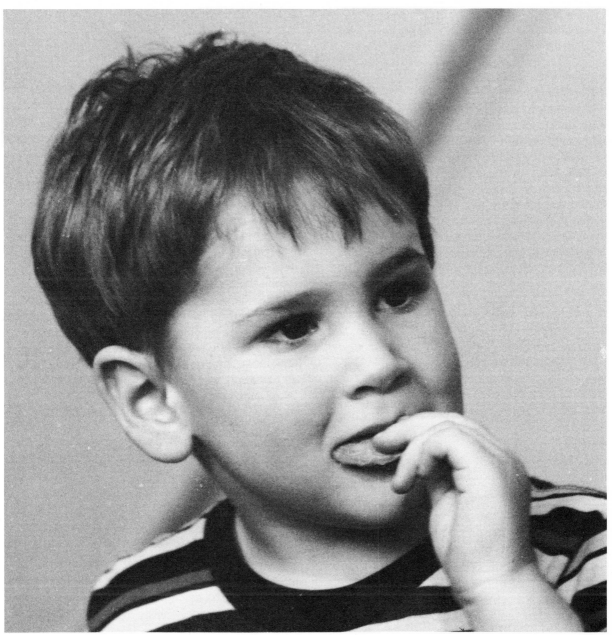

Scene from *World of Three*

instinct of self-preservation which is the most fundamental of all. In fact he begins to come apart as a human being. Man can exist as man only in relation to other men. Alone we lose the power to feel even the existence of ourselves.

All our hope of knowing ourselves is in knowing other people, but the relationship develops by knowing about the other person, since the direct knowledge we obscurely long for is not something we can get just by wanting it. This desire to know that feels its way beyond relations, that is, the knowing about, to the person himself, starts inside us within the layer where we are conscious of knowing about things. This kind of desire to know can work only by the ordinary ways of knowing about; it can work only by means of the relationship.

Rosemary Haughton, The Holiness of Sex (*Abbey Press, St. Meinrad, Indiana*), *pages 7–8.*

THE WORLD OF THREE

National Film Board of Canada

1967

28 minutes, black and white, 16mm.

Purchase: $170.00 (#34, #28); in Canada $73.00 (#77)
Rental: $8.00 (#34, #17); in Canada (#64, #68, #77)

THURSDAY'S CHILDREN

Tuesday's child is full of grace;
Wednesday's child is full of woe;
Thursday's child has far to go.

Thursday's children have far to go because they are deaf. They must learn what sound looks like, what it feels like, and transfer their sense knowledge into language. Their struggle is almost desperate and involves their survival, for only from words can their minds grow and understand adult living.

Richard Burton narrates *Thursday's Children* **with taste, and even sophisticated student audiences respond well to the children's story. The film is a documentary about the children at the Royal School for the Deaf, Margate, Britain. Since the time it was first shown in 1955, these particular children have grown and the therapeutic techniques developed for them have become dated. Nevertheless, the value of the film is that the children's deafness and their struggle for independence become symbolic of all physically underprivileged people. There is something both heroic and understated about the strength of these children and their affection for each other.**

A showing of this film would provide an opportunity to invite a handicapped person to lecture. How has his psychological and physical life differed from the lives of normal people? A report from a member of the audience concerning local conditions for the handicapped or a taped interview with a handicapped person would also be appropriate.

How did you feel as you began to become aware of the children growing?

Did you ever meet a handicapped person? How did you feel?

Compare your world with the world of the handicapped.

What do you think of the teacher? Visit a similar school for the handicapped and find out why such teachers are so dedicated.

FROM A STUDENT INTERVIEW WITH A BLIND MAN

Everybody has a handicap. What is a handicap to one is just a nuisance to another.

I had to make friends on the basis of being blind.

Then I wanted to help handicapped people overcome some of the obstacles I faced.

People react differently to their own blindness—it depends on environment and circumstances. Like any traumatic experience we face, one person may take it in stride, another might crack up.

I'd love to be able to see, but you don't worry about what you don't have—you try to work with what you've got left—the extra effort will make up for what you've lost.

And when you're working you have more—at least you're trying. What matters is the confidence others have in me and the confidence I have in myself.

The public has to be educated. Most people think handicapped people are necessarily inferior, while in reality the handicapped person may be doing more with his life than anyone. It depends on the person.

Society is losing out in this thing. There's a lot of manpower and talent going to waste.

Do I ever feel like giving up? Well, doesn't everybody at one time or another? You just do the best you can—nobody can expect more. And if you bat .500 in this thing, I think you're doing all right.

THURSDAY'S CHILDREN

British Information Services

1955

22 minutes, black and white, 16mm.

Purchase: $125.00 (#17); in Canada (#74)
Rental: $10.00 (#17, #10, #36); in Canada (#68, #64)

Narrator: Richard Burton

TELEVISION COMMERCIALS

The Museum of Modern Art in New York City distributes three twenty-minute reels of television commercials, two reels of "live" commercials, one reel of animation. The commercial, when removed from the context of television, seems to have an unusual fascination. The selections on these reels are well chosen and typical of the transferal of basic human drives to commercial objects common to advertising. Audiences seem to enjoy proving that sex, security and the good life can be associated even with bandaids.

A process analogous to the drive transferal of advertising takes place in the most sophisticated filmmaking—for example, the symbolism of Fellini or Bergman. The process also appears in experimental films like *Lines Horizontal* which relate human drives to abstract color and sound. The traditional propaganda film—for example, *The Battle of San Pietro*—follows the same principle. Audiences respond well to a comparison of these different film styles.

What motives and human needs are being stimulated to sell the products in these commercials?

What are some typical commercials and advertisements which relate their products to deep human personal needs and motives and desires? What is the relationship between the product and how it is advertised?

Make a list of commercials and advertising. Examine the visual and verbal rhetoric that links the product to the person. Do people usually recognize this connection? How much buying do you think is done by compulsion?

What effect does commercial advertising have in forming personal values?

Since most people are unconscious of the compulsive force in some advertising, do you think there should be laws protecting the person from manipulative advertising practices?

ADVERTISING: THE ART AND SCIENCE

by Joseph T. Gilbert, S.J.

Is advertising a massive plot to maneuver the helpless buyer by overwhelming appeals to his subconscious drives? Some critics imply as much. Or is it an absolutely vital part of the American economy which is so hedged in by regulations and threatened by government censorship that creativity is all but stifled? The thesis had been defended. The truth about what advertising is lies somewhere in the middle. Practically everyone, from the college *savants* to the lowest streetsweeper has an *opinion* about the nature of advertising, so it might be well to point out a few relevant facts.

Advertising is a business which has an annual expenditure in 1964 of $13.5 billion—over one-fourth of next year's defense budget. It is a business which employs hundreds of thousands of men. (J. Walter Thompson, the largest of the Madison Avenue agencies, has some 6,800 employees working in fifty-three offices all over the world.) Advertising is America's most pervasive business; "ads" are inescapably present on radio and television, subway, bus, billboard, newspaper, and magazine.

Informative Persuasion

Advertising has a two-fold purpose: to inform potential buyers that a producer has a product or service for sale, and to persuade the buyers to purchase this commodity here and now. The function of advertising, therefore, in the total economic system which is American free enterprise, is not manufacturing, nor transporting, nor even a sales transaction. It is the business that effects a meeting of minds between buyer and seller.

The most important and well known of the two functions of advertising is its role as persuader. Except for a few carefully planned instances, an advertisement does not merely state that Yellow Cab has a lot of taxies, or that Budweiser has a lot of beer in the brewery. Many of the basic differences of opinion among professionals arise over the question of means of persuasion. As we shall see, there are two schools of thought. This is also the area which draws the most complaints from audiences.

The principal vehicles of modern advertising are the mass media—a conveniently vague term which nowadays means more and more a media that can attract a nationwide audience. Even a moderately popular evening television show may draw a national audience in the millions; *TV Guide, Life* and *Look* each have weekly circulations in excess of seven million; there are some eighteen hundred daily newspapers in the United States, and almost as many radios as people.

The costs of advertising reach some astronomical figures of their own. Fifty thousand dollars will buy an ad on the back cover of *Life* (one issue), and a network spectacular during television's prime evening hours may sell for a quarter of a billion dollars. Advertisers, it seems, are convinced of the effectiveness of mass media ads.

Results

Given the medium, what makes an ad effective? "Eye-catching" is the first criterion. In local grocery ads this is no problem: housewives avidly scan these pages looking for one-day specials on veal or peanut butter with "ten cents off." In the movie section of a daily paper the eye-catcher is frequently blatant sex appeal, which may or may not have much to do with the theme of the movie. On television an ad becomes "dead space" unless it starts well, time for discussing the program or dashing to the kitchen for a quick beer. As for radio, we are all familiar with the transistor audience that switches stations if the ads aren't as "swingin' " as the top forty. In a magazine the challenge is even greater; the best copy ever written will be passed over unless the eye-catcher is unique. Only a few companies have really mastered the art of the unique; who, for example, can ignore a large white space with a tiny picture of a Volkswagen in one corner, and the caption, "Think Small"?

Once the attention is arrested, the battle is half won, but the remaining half is a challenge in itself. The appeal must be interesting and convincing. The key is to tie one's product to some need, desire, or value of the audience. There are two basic techniques to accomplish this. The traditional approach for many years has been to arrange a direct confrontation between a known need and a known product. This is still widely used today, as, for example, in motel signs along the highways. When modern psychology brought to the world an acute awareness of subconscious attitudes, needs, and desires, it also brought a revolution in advertising. To what extent persuasion should be directed toward the subconscious is one of the most vital and hotly disputed questions ever to face the advertising business. The issue is one of both ethics and effectiveness. In neither case have solid norms been established.

Fact or Fancy

At present the difference in approaches seems based in agency preferences. Some agencies and departments make considerable use of psychologists, sociologists, and motivational researchers. Others remain aloof from this whole approach, preferring to stress plain facts about their product. In advertising a new car, for example, the former emphasizes such factors as status symbol (Cadillac and foreign makes are high status), the masculine aggressiveness of a high-powered engine, and sex appeal (have you seen a Dodge ad recently?). The latter, such as the advertisers of Willys stationwagon, stress structural safety, low operating costs, and durability. Toothpastes furnish another example of the double approach. Gleem has made itself famous by plugging a scientific ingredient—GL-70. Stripe, on the other hand, takes the psychological approach and finds considerable success in telling its audience how much fun it is to brush with a toothpaste that has a red, peppermint stripe.

One of the most amazing facts about advertising is that it is impossible to measure its results. In the long range, a company can compare sales and advertising expenditures, of course, but when Coca-Cola, for example, spends the fifty thousand dollars for a full-page ad on the back cover of one issue of *Life,* they have no way of knowing if this ad sold fifty dollars or fifty thousand dollars worth of Coke. This problem led to the origin and growth of an important stepchild of advertising—market research. The function of market research is to calculate as accurately as possible the effectiveness of advertising, to foresee trends among consumers and to suggest changes and innovations among advertisers. How recent and rapid advances in this field have been can be gathered from the article by Mr. John Henderson. Needless to say, this area of advertising is still in its pioneer stages.

While measurement of advertising results is very rough at best, the $13.5 million annual advertising budget betrays a rather large faith in the effectiveness of the art. Just to keep "Madison Avenue" humble, there does exist at least one company which defies all the theories. Hershey sells a very large amount of chocolate, and just when did you last see a Hershey bar advertised?

Responsibility

When one has finished speaking of advertising in general, he must come back to the fact that advertising is the work of individual men and women. To forget this is to pave the way for moral buck-passing. What good will one protest do if an objectionable ad is the work of an impersonal colossus? Still worse, men actually in the business may leave moral decisions to "others." Recently in a general circulation magazine, there was an ad for a certain skin lotion. It showed an unclothed model lying on a dark-colored carpet; the tone of the article was blatantly sexual. The caption read "Keep your birthday suit wrinkle-free." The moral implications of this sort of advertising are questionable at best. Who is responsible—the manufacturer? the advertising agency? the magazine? the audience who accepts this type of thing? In reality, the individuals all along the line are responsible.

Advertising is serious business. Its physical presence almost everywhere we turn needs no emphasis, but the effect it has on our ideas and ideals, our principles and practices is a matter deserving serious consideration. As psychology makes more evident the profound influence on our whole way of thinking which something as pervasive as advertising achieves, the importance of giving this field more than passing consideration becomes evident. Political advertising is a matter of no small import. The effects of advertising on the moral climate of America cannot be ignored. The possibilities of creative and artistic expression through advertising hold out considerable promise. The ethical propriety of some experimental techniques needs exploration. Interest in advertising, then, is not merely for the professionals in the field and the professors of economics and business, it is for every man in a position of responsibility, for every teacher of youth, and indeed, for every mature, thinking individual.

From Enterprise, *Jan. 1965, 3700 West Pine Boulevard, St. Louis, Mo., 63108*

TELEVISION COMMERCIALS

Film Department

Museum of Modern Art

1963–66

Reels 1, 2, 3—20 minutes each; black and white and color together, 16mm.
Reel 1—13 Commercials
Reel 2—18 Commercials
Reel 3—16 Commercials

Purchase: can't buy
Rental: $10.00 per reel (#31)

APPENDIX FOR FREEDOM

A trumpet for the Combo
Hutterites
Gandhi
Time Piece
Automania 2000
My Own Back Yard To Play In
Science Friction
Triumph of the Will

Related material: For readings on Freedom confer DISCOVERY IN WORD, pages 27–54

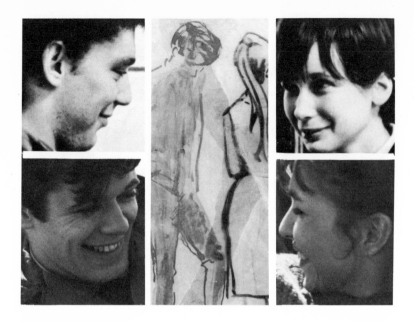

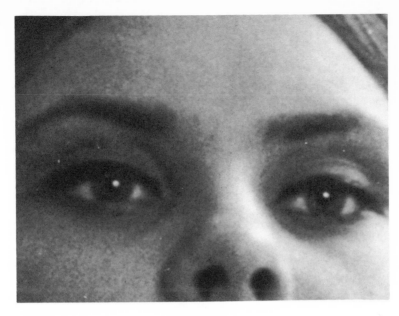

LOVE

The Most
The Game
Phoebe
Merry-Go-Round
A Quarter Million Teenagers
You're No Good
Time Piece
Overture
In the Name of God
The Soldier
The Lord Is My Shepherd
Nativity of Jesus Christ

THE MOST

Hugh Hefner and his Playboy philosophy have become a standard for some and a matter of satire for others. *The Most* **is a brilliant satirical documentary. Ballentine and Sheppard, the producers of the film, gained access to Hefner's home, office and partying life. They simply record what they see and hear—and edit. Their comment is a must for any discussion of contemporary epicureanism.**

What were your reactions to Hugh Hefner as you watched this documentary?

What did you admire in the persons at the Playboy mansion? What attitudes did you find inadequate?

Judging from the film techniques, how did the producers, Gordon Sheppard and Richard Ballentine, evaluate the Playboy way of life?

What do you think of the life vision of Hugh Hefner?

Why do you think this film is entitled The Most?

Do you think the Playboy philosophy has been successful in the United States? Why? Or, why not? What is the Playboy view of woman? What are Hugh Hefner's views on the significance of sex? Is it possible to see a new type of "Victorianism" in his attitude? What are your own values concerning sex?

Do you think Hugh Hefner would allow his daughter to become a bunny (cf. interview in Look 1/10/67 in reference to this question)?

Would you appreciate seeing your college senior son or your father going to a "bunny club"? Why? Or, why not?

LOVE AND SEX

Sexuality might well be said to be at the base of civilized life. I think it was John Galsworthy who said that culture began when the first protohuman female turned around to face her lover during sex. When one looks at the cultures in which great achievements and advances in the arts, humane arrangements of everyday life, and kindliness have been made, one finds that they are usually cultures where romantic love and the private relationship between one man and one woman have been glorified. Where women are merely the physiological utensils of men, civilization is usually a poor thing. Creativity seems to be greatest in societies where extraordinary feats of private emotion are achievable and even laudable.

If one takes cultures where romantic love is regarded as a kind of disease, as in, say, traditional Japanese culture, one finds something missing. A kind of feeling—maybe the word for it is tenderness —is absent. The old Japanese culture had all kinds of sensitivity but not, I think, tenderness. The delicacy of feeling between one person and another, which in its social consequences becomes a profound compassion among a people, exists most richly in cultures where the emotional penumbra of sexual experience is richest.

Romantic sexual love, at its best, requires a balance between the idealistic—or whatever one chooses to call the sense that life is a metaphor— and the sensual. Renaissance Italy had it, and so did Elizabethan England. It also demands fairly clear notions of masculinity and femininity, and respect and admiration of both. Arabic culture, for example, seems stagnant and profoundly lacking; and I suspect this is because the Arabs lack a sense that women have a peculiar, adorable, and equal quality.

From "Sex, Love, and Modern Education," by Donald Barr, Columbia College Today, *Fall 1967, page 36.*

THE MOST

Gordon Sheppard and Richard Ballentine
Toronto

1962

28 minutes, black and white, 16mm.

Purchase: inquire (#26); in Canada (#72)
Rental: inquire (#26); in Canada (#67)

Producer and Director: Gordon Sheppard and
Richard Ballentine

Awards

Grand Prize 1962
Mannheim Festival of Documentary Films

First Prize for Documentary 1962
San Francisco

First Prize tie with *The Fat and The Lean*
Melbourne Festival

THE GAME

Peter is challenged by his peer group to play
the serio-comic teenage game of girl-baiting. He
meets Nicky, and their game relationship leads to the
reality of intercourse. *The Game* concludes after
Peter and Nicky have developed the beginning of
adult awareness.

The camera technique in *The Game* simulates a
teenage mood with its oddly angled shots and sudden
transitions. Amusing camera selectivity emphasizes
the adolescent sensitivity to sex, and later in the film,
silence, shadow and long held distance shots achieve
a touching consciousness of guilt. The sound track
frequently overlaps shot and sequence transitions
and contributes to the atmosphere of sudden event
and excitement.

The Game is best discussed in mixed company
—boys and girls together, or, better, adults with
teenagers.

*What does love mean to Peter? Do you think he is
afraid to love? Do you think he is afraid to be loved?*

*Peter is pressured by his group. How does this
pressure form his values? Does this justify Peter's
activity?*

How typical is Peter in his actions?

*"That's what they said you'd do." How true is Nicky's
comment about Peter?*

*Is Peter's attitude toward school—"Work the
minimum; get the maximum"—very common? Why?*

*Would you describe Peter as a sensitive person?
Why? Or, why not?*

*When he returns to his gang, has Peter's attitude
changed?*

*What is the "game"? What are its rules? What is
the prize?*

*What kind of a game does Peter play with his parents
and his school? Does Nicky play a similar game?*

*Does the director George Kaczander play a game
with his audience by shot selection and other film
techniques?*

*Is the use of the drill symbol at the end of the film
too startling and obvious? As the film progresses,
what does Kaczander gain by shooting many of his*

Scene from *The Game*

shots with a drummer in the foreground? How does he make use of phone conversations in this film?

Related material: refer to Alfie *in DISCOVERY IN SONG (Glen Rock, N.J.: Paulist Press, 1968), page 71.*

STUDENTS' COMMENTARY ON *THE GAME*

"It was true to life. More than that I really can't say. The movie speaks for itself. It is truly a masterpiece."

"*The Game* is typical of many of today's youth, myself included. Many times you hear of people doing it, and it ends right there. Not often do you hear of a guy getting stuck."

"Peter is an adolescent and a virgin. At his age, and our age, virginity is often a demerit pointing against the individual. The 'game' is to prove his manhood by losing his virginity. His friends encourage him, and his ego demands that he become a player. Nicky is the other player—or, perhaps, the victim. Peter, on a dare, makes love to her and then leaves her, just as the rules state. He finds himself unable to stick to these rules, however, and calls her, finding more in her than he wanted or expected."

"It shows us what can happen if we let our instincts take preference over our morals."

"Unlike other films of this nature that usually keep forcing God and religion on you, this film shows just these people and how the 'game' can be overcome by yourself."

"I wish that they would show or express the girl's sentiments or feelings on what she's out for on a date."

"A very realistic film. I could understand the feeling of both Peter and Nicky, also the pressures of the crowd."

"Nicky was insecure and Peter was overconfident. Together this made a bad combination."

"*The Game* is an extreme rendition of the 'Playboy' philosophy gauged down to the adolescent. . . ."

"Once in such a serious situation most boys would try to repent as Peter did, but few would have the guts to follow through with it."

"The one point that did come across very clearly is that Peter was very foolish to have been led on by his friends, and in the end he realized that he had made a very bad mistake."

THE GAME

National Film Board of Canada

1967

28 minutes, black and white, 16mm.

Purchase: $170.00 (#34, #17); in Canada $73.00 (#77)
Rental: $8.00 (#17, #27); in Canada (#64, #68, #77)

Director: George Kaczander
Producer: John Kemeny

PHOEBE

The adolescent feminine sexual psychology is markedly more subtle than the male's. As *The Game* examined the male psychology in an adolescent premarital sexual relationship, *Phoebe* is a classic study of the female.

Phoebe attempts to communicate the fact that she is pregnant to Paul, her boyfriend. She is tortured by her own perception of herself as evil, and she is frightened by the possibility of rejection. In a series of flashbacks, Phoebe not only relives her experiences with Paul, but envisions the assorted possible reactions of her parents, the school authorities and Paul to her pregnancy. Paul is not sensitive and does not want to listen to Phoebe—she tries and cannot communicate with him. At the conclusion of the film, she calls Paul on the telephone, tells him of her pregnancy in one phrase, hangs up and cries.

What beyond the obvious pregnancy is Phoebe's problem? What, if anything, is Paul's problem?

Of all Phoebe's conjectures about the reactions of her parents when they find out, what does she think they most likely will do?

What are Phoebe's parents' roles and relations to each other?

What is the position of the principal of her school most likely going to be?

Why did Phoebe reject Paul when he finally realized that something was wrong and asked her to tell him what it was?

Would you say that the attitude of the girl at the party speaking about her abortion was helpful or mature?

What is the significance of the threesome at the other end of the beach—their dancing around and their remoteness?

Why does Phoebe finally tell Paul over the phone? What would you do if faced with such a situation?

In the film No Reason To Stay, *the girl Joan tells her boyfriend, Chris Wood, that it's silly to wait. What possible responses to Joan's statement does this film provoke?*

Related material: refer to DISCOVERY IN SONG, Georgy Girl, page 76.

HOW DO YOU DECIDE?

One basis for decision-making is possible *outcome.* In your own experience, what happens as a result of premarital sexual relations? To your knowledge, what are the chances of something good coming out of such behavior? Something bad? How good? How bad? What reliable evidence is there that you can base your judgment on? Are you acquainted with the findings of valid research on this question? Have you talked over the problem with an informed responsible person who knows you and what you are deciding?

Your decision should be based upon possible outcome in terms of your own sense of what is appropriate. Since there are many life styles, and many kinds of persons, each must resolve the issue in terms of his or her own values and self concept. . . .

A second basis for moral decision is that of *universality.* Ask yourself what would it be like if everyone did just what he or she felt like. If every boy took any girl who was available, what kind of world would it be? If couples engaged freely in premarital intercourse, what assurance would they have of fidelity after they married? If husbands and

Scene from *Phoebe*

wives were not faithful to each other, what kind of family life would result? How could a man be sure his children were his? How could either of them feel permanently secure in their life together? Would women, would men, be better off or worse? Would marriages be happier or under more strain? How would children fare? What kind of culture would result? Does sexual restraint make a stronger or a weaker society?

A third basis for developing premarital sex standards is *cultural*. Dr. Leuba suggests that a culture in which premarital sexual intercourse would be desirable and satisfactory would have to meet the following conditions:

1. If guilt and shame were not associated with premarital sex expression in childhood-upbringing.

2. If there were no social disapproval either for the persons engaging in premarital sexual relations or for the institutions of which they were members.

3. If young people reaching puberty were well informed regarding the basic male and female sexual makeup and regarding socially acquired sexual attitudes.

4. If privacy were readily available; and sexual functioning were successfully restricted within satisfactory limits.

5. If universal and competent training in contraception were available.

6. If young people were brought up to take sex neither too seriously nor too lightly.

7. If social life were such that it would be easy for women as well as for men to become well acquainted with many members of the opposite sex, so that a woman, for instance, who had lost a partner would be able to find a new and equally satisfactory one without being left stranded or drifting into promiscuity.

8. If venereal diseases were rare or nonexistent.

9. If provisions were made for the care of offspring.

We would add to this listing three further conditions:

10. If religious teachings approved of premarital and extramarital sexual relationships.

11. If human-development findings indicated that adolescent sex experience encourages the full development of the personality of both partners.

12. If premarital sexual conduct promoted the development of the family and the culture.

A reviewer would be optimistic indeed to convince himself that these conditions are being met in America today! Go down the listing yourself and see whether you can honestly appraise any of these twelve conditions necessary for premarital sexual intercourse as being met here and now.

E. M. Duvall, Why Wait Till Marriage?, *Association Press*

PHOEBE

National Film Board of Canada

1965

28 minutes, black and white, 16mm.

Purchase: $160.00 (#28, #34); in Canada $73.00 (#77)
Rental: $8.00 (#17, #27); in Canada (#64, #68, #77)

Writer and Director: George Kaczander
Producer: Julian Biggs
Photography: Paul Leach
Music: Robert Fleming
Dialog: Noel Stone

Awards

Blue Ribbon Award, Guidance Category

American Film Festival 1966
New York, New York

Diploma of Merit, Short Film Competition
Melbourne Film Festival
Melbourne, Australia 1966

MERRY-GO-ROUND

Merry-Go-Round **follows no story line. It is a discussion film about sex presenting the opinions of a leading educator, Mary Winspear, psychotherapist Albert Ellis, and newspaper columnist Ann Landers. The style of the film, with its quick-cut, merry-go-round rhythm, shapes their rapid discussion method and moves suddenly from one point of view to another. Each participant differs in outlook. Miss Landers is conservative, Dr. Ellis is extremely liberal, and Mrs. Winspear is indecisively somewhere inbetween.** *Merry-Go-Round* **has an advantage in its lack of story line: it brings its audience immediately to the point of controversy.**

MERRY-GO-ROUND

"Sex means love; it means giving; often it means motherhood. . . ."

"Sex is great; it's a driving biological impelled force. . . ."

"Sex is marvelous, *the* great force. . . ."
I. Guitar Scene

"I think there is a profound sex revolution in attitudes and behavior among young people."

"I think boys and girls are both engaging in sexual activity at a rate never before known in the history of mankind."

"It seems to me that teenagers today are using sex: girls are using it to get the sort of pleasure they want—dates and so on; boys seem to be using it to establish their virility."

"I'm concerned because there seems to be a decline in moral standards—a great many teenagers don't think anything of going all the way. . . ."

"It seems to me very sad, guilt-ridden, fear-ridden. . . ."

"I think they're having much less guilt about engaging in such sex relations as petting and intercourse. . . ."
Is there a sex revolution?
Do girls use sex to lure boys?
Do boys use sex to establish their virility?
Is there a decline in moral standards?
What about fear, guilt, and sex activity?
II. Skiing Scene

The taboo on sex activity goes back to ancient times. Do you think "vested socio-economic interests" are the reasons why things don't change?

"Boys and girls think differently about sex activity." Would you agree?

"It is wise for a girl to realize she must have a deeper relationship." What is this "deeper" personal relationship?

What are the problems involved in developing a "deeper personal relationship" between a teenage boy and girl? Is a "deep personal" relationship between teenagers different by nature from a deep personal relationship between adults? Are there separate codes for each age group?
III. Car-after-Movie Scene

"Sex belongs in marriage." What do you think?

"Teenagers should be encouraged to pet to climax." What would you teach your daughter?

"Don't if you don't have to." Would you agree? Why?

"Sex without good emotions and spiritual relationship is like sneezing." What is a good emotional relationship for a teenager? What is an

Scene from *Merry-Go-Round*

emotional relationship that would make one less a person?

IV. Sex-in-American-Life Scene

As we witness the sexy magazines and images—the signs of society's lessons on sex—the psychotherapist says: "I would like to see sex portrayed as a good thing, not as nasty, indecent and bad."

How does society's teachings on sex mold our personal attitudes? How would you present sex so that it would be a constructive influence in the public life?

V. Girls-at-Lunch Scene

"Your decision has nothing to do with your parents." In what way is this true? How is it false?

Her girl friend encourages her: "I did it. Nothing is wrong with me." In the situation is this a strong influence?

VI. Strip-Show Scene

"[The] double standard is disappearing." Do you agree?

What does the film director say about the boys' sex attitude in this scene?

VII. Peter's Room Scene

"Sex has purpose. Sex says 'I love you.' " How does sex say this?

"Sex requires maturity, responsibility—which at the age of puberty children don't have." Would you agree?

"[Sex between an] immature boy and immature girl results in a stultifying relationship." How would this happen? What are the effects of a "stultifying relationship"?

VIII. Standing at the Window: Closeout Scene

"Accept your sexuality. Realize its power . . . control it." How is sexuality productive, beautiful and wisely experienced by the teenager?

A person has a choice and is different from mating animals. "Choose and then hope, hope for the best." How is my choosing related to my sexual activity? What do you hope *for* yourself? What do you hope *for* the other person? What do you hope *from* the other person? Does hope form your sexual attitudes?

Does the rapid change of pictures at the end of the film have anything to do with the "merry-go-round"?

Related material: refer to Discovery in Song, *"Sitting on a Fence," page 75*

MERRY-GO-ROUND

National Film Board of Canada

1967

23 minutes, black and white, 16mm.

Purchase: $140.00 (#28, #34); in Canada $60.00 (#77)
Rental: $6.00 (#17, #27); in Canada (#64, #68, #77)

Tania Valentine

A QUARTER MILLION TEENAGERS

A Quarter Million Teenagers **is an instructional film about syphilis and gonorrhea, known generally as venereal disease or VD. It presents the biological data surrounding venereal disease and explains its effect. The film is clear and well made, and although its purpose is to instruct teenagers in the recognition and treatment of venereal disease, it can stimulate frank discussion about the fear and guilt so often harmfully present with sexual experiences.**

Why is the rate of VD so much higher among teenagers?

Scene from *A Quarter Million Teenagers*

If it is so easily treated, why doesn't everyone go readily for treatment?

Should one with VD be ashamed? Why? Or, why not?

Is guilt the same as shame?

In this matter are guilt feelings good or bad? What would the sources of these feelings be?

Why would you feel it necessary to make such a film?

A QUARTER MILLION TEENAGERS

Churchill Films
(In cooperation with Los Angeles City Schools and L.A. County Health Dist.)

1964

16 minutes, color, 16mm.
Spanish version available

Purchase: $180.00 (#13); in Canada $190.00 (#69)
Rental: $10.00 (#13); in Canada (#76, #68, #64, #69)

YOU'RE NO GOOD

You're No Good **is the story of a teenager as he runs and hides from the police. Eddie stole a motorbike in order to show off to his girlfriend and to project reality into his unfulfilled dream of success. This dream world is conveyed through a system of frequently humorous fantasy shots interpolated into the text of Eddie's story.**

The motivation for Eddie's flight evolved from his entire social context. Eddie was humiliated by his every contact with the established and successful world. He was lonely and jealous of his girlfriend and secretly proud that the police were looking for him, that someone cared. Most viewers of *You're No Good* **will not be as acutely in trouble as Eddie, yet they will be able to identify with the general problems with communication and acceptance that he symbolizes.**

How did you feel as you watched Eddie confront himself? What do you think were Eddie's feelings? What did you like most about Eddie?

What did the bike mean to Eddie as he contemplated taking it?

Eddie told his friends not to say they saw him. They did not say anything either to the social worker or to the police. Would you agree with their action? Suppose they knew telling the social worker would be helping Eddie in the long run—do you think they would have spoken to the social worker?

Contrast Eddie's dreaming about his girl and their confrontation at the social club. What do you think about his girl? Do you think his girl-dreaming is ordinary?

Describe Eddie's relationship with his mother and his father.

Which lines from the songs caught the mood of the scene? What are some songs that match your moods well?

Eddie dreams of himself as a star singer, as an ace pool player, as a romantic lover. Do you think this is typical of a teenager? Do you think it is helpful for growing?

Why did he feel like throwing a hand grenade at the office building?

He shouts several times: "Get me out of here" as he bangs on the walls of the huge empty room. What was this scene all about?

Why choose the title You're No Good?

How do you learn to have empathy for someone like Eddie?

Related material: refer to DISCOVERY IN SONG, Nowhere Man, *pages 18–19*

A PEARL OF A GIRL

Do you remember that sensitive motion picture *David and Lisa*? It told the story of two emotionally disturbed adolescents. At one point in the picture, Lisa asks David, "What do you see when you see me?" This is a typical question of any adolescent, not only one who is emotionally disturbed. Adolescents are trying to find out who they are by looking into other people's eyes to see their own reflection. They use their peers and adults as mirrors.

When he was asked by Lisa, "What do you see when you see me?" David answered, "I see a pearl of a girl." Every adolescent is hoping to hear something like that repeated frequently. Because this is an emotional appreciation of something, it can be repeated again and again. It is not sufficient to say,

"I told you yesterday that your work was splendid." They want to hear you say it every day. They are forever seeking to identify themselves in you, and yet they change so fast, even in one day, that it is difficult to respond to them. You feel like saying, "Who are you now?" They can't tell you who they are because they are trying to find out. . . .

The bathroom mirror is also a good place for trying on faces. Now the face is sophisticated, now arrogant, now pensive or aloof. Because it is so difficult for us to regress to the point that we can remember what it felt like to be fourteen years old, much of the behavior of adolescents strikes us as being very funny. There is no humor in it for the young man or woman. It is an extremely painful time of life. He is trying to discover his real self. There are so many roles possible for him to try on. He fears he will never find his real self.

From Teenage, *J. McCall, S.J., M. Link, S.J. and R. Leach (Argus Communications Co. 3505 N. Ashland Ave., Chicago, Ill. 60657), pp. 10–11*

A HOUSE OF STRANGERS

Whether he is a crusader or a conformist, whether he is committed or plays it cool, whether he is apathetic or involved, whether he has hope or whether he has "cut out," the young stranger who dwells in the house of our republic is very likely to do lip service to and, indeed, even to sincerely profess at least four notions.

First of all, he is profoundly committed to the idea that the human person represents the most important value in the world. He distrusts ideologies, panaceas, utopias, concrete programs. He believes profoundly in the importance of human relations and the necessity of love (though he might not always be sure of his own capacity for love). He may not have

Scene from *You're No Good*

read any existentialist philosophy books, may only know dimly the names of existentialist novels, but his whole style of behavior is existentialist and personalist. He views his future happiness as being essentially relational whether it be in the secure domesticity of a suburban escape or in the total commitment of the civil rights organizer.

Secondly, he distrusts organizations, largely because most of the organizations which he has experienced in his life have, he feels, cheated him of the spontaneity and honesty in his relationships. He may well fall for the phony communities provided by the totalitarian concept of participatory democracy, but he does so because such forms of tyranny appear to him to be unorganized and organization is presumed to be evil until the contrary is proven. Indeed, many young people even refuse to concede the possibility that any organization could be good, at least for very long, and they may find reinforcement from the writings of their elders who look forward eagerly to an "institutionless community" without realizing that such words are self-contradictory.

Thirdly, the young person rejects tradition. It is inconceivable that he can learn anything from the past, its history, its mistakes, its wisdom, its insights. Those who have gone before him have made a complete mess of the world and their lives and have nothing to offer him. He must start over anew and rebuild the world. . . .

Finally, while the young American may be very articulate in his criticisms and rejections of the world of the past and the disorganization of the present, his own descriptions of what he wants out of life are very inarticulate, whether they be idealistic or hedonistic. He knows what he doesn't want, but he's not at all sure what he wants. He knows where he is not going with his life, but his descriptions of

where he is going are either terribly dull or terribly confused. It seems that his society has given him everything a young person could want except goals, norms, values, and clear vision.

From Strangers in the House *by Andrew M. Greely,* © *Sheed and Ward, Inc., 1961*

YOU'RE NO GOOD

National Film Board of Canada

1965

28 minutes, black and white, 16mm.

Purchase: $160.00 (#34, #28); in Canada $87.00 (#77)
Rental: $8.00 (#17, #34); in Canada (#77, #68, #64)

Director: George Kaczander
Producer: Julian Biggs

TIME PIECE

Time Piece **comments on the traps which enclose the ordinary person in an ordinary life. At the beginning of the film, a man waits in a hospital room and listens to the rhythmic signal of his heart. It becomes for him the signal of pursuit, the measure of time passing, the ratrace of business and the monotony of every day. He reflects on his life and calls out for help from within a dollar bill, a serving platter and a toilet bowl—the symbols of his trapped situation. At the conclusion of the film, someone draws a sheet over the man's body. The camera angles upward, and we see that it is the same man who was in bed and who is now leaving behind his former life.**

Time Piece was shot at a ratio of seventy to one. For every foot of film incorporated in its final length, seventy feet were photographed. This is seven times the normal commercial ratio. *Time Piece* is a concentrated satire on modern living well worth discussing.

Did you recognize any single theme in this film? What did the symbols you noticed point to?

What were the symbols of joy, of monotony, of relevancy and of frustration in this film?

Within the dollar, on the food platter, while flying, and in the toilet, the man in the film cries "Help!" How does it feel to be trapped in such situations? What causes one to be trapped like this? How does a person grow or decline in such circumstances?

Create your own expression of "your time"—in song, in poetry, in film, in pictures.

Related material: refer to DISCOVERY IN SONG, A Day in the Life, page 133.

CHANGES

by Phil Ochs (Phil Ochs in Concert—
Electra Records EKS7310)

Sit by my side, come as close as the air, share in a
    memory
of gray and wander in my words and dream about
    the pictures I play
of changes
Green leaves of summer turn red in the fall, to brown
    and to
yellow they fade

And then they have to die, trapped within the circle
    time parade
of changes
Scenes of my young years were warm in my mind,
    visions of shadows that shined
Till one day I returned and found they were victims
    of the line
of changes
The world spinning madly, it drifts in the dark, and
    swings
through a hollow of haze
A race around the sun, a journey through a universe
    of lace
with changes
Moments of magic will grow in the night, all fears of
    the forest
are gone
But when the morning breaks they're swept away by
    the golden
drops of dawn
and changes
Passions will part to a strange melody, as fires will
    sometimes
grow cold
Like petals in the wind, we're puppets to the silver
    strings of soul
and changes
Your tears will be trembling, now we're somewhere
    else, one
last cup of wine we will pour
And I'll kiss you one more time and leave you on the
    rolling
river shore
of changes

TIME PIECE

Muppets, Inc. Production

1965

8 minutes, color, 16mm.

Purchase: $135.00 (#17); in Canada (#74)
Rental: $15.00 (#17, #27)

Directed by Jim Henson

OVERTURE

Shots of harvest time and natural wealth, shots of loneliness and war, and shots of planting and rebuilding compose an initial triptych in *Overture* and state a theme of cyclic process. Gradually a new theme emerges, the vision of man helping man. Man himself, *Overture* seems to be saying, can reach into the natural order and rearrange it, can be responsible for his future, can help by service to create a world of empathy. The United Nations is presented as a light to the world which can indeed turn swords into plowshares and the inevitable cyclic pattern into a more linear progress.

The United Nations may be forgiven its largely written signature in *Overture* both because of the high quality of the film and because the United Nations should itself become the topic of discussion. Many Americans have slipped into pessimism with regard to the place of the United Nations in world affairs. Is the United Nations philosophy as presented in *Overture*, with its obviously Christian optimism, unattainable?

From this film what did you see as the main problems of the world?

What are the signs and dimensions of poverty in the world today? Choose a particular Asian, Latin American or African country and compare its vital statistics (GNP, infant mortality, life span, rate of illiteracy, number of physicians and hospitals, diet) with those of the United States.

Act out a dialog between poverty and hope in the future as spoken by an American citizen and a citizen from the country chosen in the previous question.

What do you think is the purpose of the United Nations? What is the role of the United States in the United Nations? What are attitudes of world leaders toward the U.N.? Of Mao Tsetung? Of Pope Paul VI?

Report on the agencies of the UN which are related to the problems of world poverty. What have these agencies accomplished?

What part could you play in combating the evils of world poverty?

POVERTY IN THE WORLD

30% of the world population living in Europe and North America owns 80% of the world's wealth, while 70% in Africa, Asia and Latin America own 20%.

Between 300 and 450 million people are underfed in the world today; 50% of the world's population suffers from malnutrition.

Signs of poverty in the world:
Hunger

15,000 die of starvation a day, 10,000 of them children. 40 million die annually of hunger and malnutrition.

Life Span

England: 68; France: 63; Egypt: 35; India: 32. Infant mortality rate in poor nations: 70 per 1,000; in rich nations: 5 per 1,000.

Illiteracy

Over 50% of the children of the world have no chance for a formal education. 50% of the people in Latin America over 6 years of age are illiterate.

Sickness

The number of physicians in the poor countries is extremely low; in some there is only one doctor for 100,000 people. The frustration is compounded by the lack of medical facilities.

What is happening to alleviate this grave problem? Tragically, the world economic situation is such that the rich nations continue to get richer and the poor nations poorer. 25% of the world's population is always moving forward, while the remaining 75% has been going backward. The per capita Gross National Product in the U.S. went from $3,500 (1966) to $3,640 (1967), while in India, Brazil and Nigeria it went from $150 to $156. This widening gap is aggravated by the population growth —14 million a year for rich nations, 44 million for poor nations—and by the draining of talented people away from the poor nations. One important source of economic growth is investment. But investment in the poor nations by the rich ones is determined by the profit motive. The United States invested more in Belgium in 1965 than in all the poor countries put together. Factors also affecting the situation are (1) spending 70 billion dollars yearly on war, (2) decrease in foreign aid, and

(3) the increase of savings of American people— 1,000 billion dollars.

Almost 99% of the world's Christians live in the rich nations of the world!

From One Fifth of the Nation *by E. Greenwood. National Council of Churches.*

A CRUCIAL WORLD PROBLEM

Tears and anger generally mark the psychology of these young nations which suffer from a new ailment, unnoticed at first and which is now unbearable— an awareness of the economic and civil imbalance which cuts them off from and humiliates them when compared to prosperous nations.

It is a crucial and worldwide problem. It transfers the well-known social question from within the individual societies to an international level, to all of humanity. If social justice (which promotes advancement of the classes which make up a society toward a more equitable distribution of the wealth and of culture, so that no one shall lack sufficient means to live as a man should, and no one shall have an immoderate and egotistical enjoyment of temporal goods while others are painfully lacking in them) is applied on the plane of relations between one nation and another, it is possible to understand the vast extent and importance of the problems arising from modern progress, when, today, every nation knows about it, and, knowing about it, claims to take part in it. And, from many points of view it is a legitimate claim.

Could the Church fail to take an interest in this gigantic aspect of contemporary human life? The Church, surely, is not expected to occupy itself with the technical solution of these problems: this is to say, with the economic and political problems having to do with admittance of peoples undergoing development to the level of sufficiency and dignity which pertains to them. These very problems, however, derive their logical and human strength from a concept of human life which only religion can give them.

In other words, it is religion, and the Christian religion above all, which sees in human progress a divine intention. God created man so that he might be lord of the earth and that the earth might be for the orderly benefit of all. It is religion which offers a basis of justice to the claims of the have-nots, when it reminds us that all men are sons of the same heavenly Father and therefore are brothers.

It is religion alone which can call on one who is rich to be an administrator and not a despotic master of his holdings, the fruits of which must in some equitable measure be to the advantage of those who are in need of them.

Pope Paul VI, Address to General Audience, March 27, 1968 (quoted from The Advocate, *Topic Section, May 1968, p. 6)*

OVERTURE

United Nations

1958

9 minutes, black and white, 16mm.

Purchase: $45.00 (#17); in Canada $33.00 (#77)
Rental: $4.00 (#17, #10, #42); in Canada (#77, #64, #68)

Awards

Academy Award Nominee, Documentary Short Subjects 1958

IN THE NAME OF GOD

In the Name of God is an ABC News Special about four missionaries: Rev. Edmund Kalan, a Lutheran clergyman of the Caroline-Marshall Islands; Rev. Hugh Costigan, S.J., a Roman Catholic priest from Ponape in the Caroline-Marshall Islands; Rev. Gifford H. Towle, a minister of the United Church of Christ in Western India; and Rev. Vincent Ferrer, S.J., a Roman Catholic priest, also of India.

While familiarizing the viewer with the work of these men, *In the Name of God* presents through them the modern missionary rationale. The Christian missionary today is one of the strongest forces teaching underdeveloped peoples to come to terms with the poverty and cultural lack of identity which the more affluent world has forced upon them. If the missionary's ultimate objective is to make God more fully present to his people, this theological goal is closely identified with the missionary's economic and cultural work. Father Ferrer formulates this relationship:

"We do not want to change the customs or the culture of India. After all, India has got a civilization that is thousands of years old, and the social customs and the personality they have are very rich. The richness of their culture and their social customs has to be enriched precisely by raising their living standards. We don't want to convert people, to change their religion. After all, Christian religion is the religion of love. What we are going there for is to love people. And this love has to be put into action."

How did you feel as you shared the experiences of these Christian missionaries? What do you think about such men who dedicate their lives to mission

*work in such places as India and Micronesia? Are
they happy? Why? Why not?*

*How did Father Costigan, Reverend Towle and
Father Ferrer interpret Christ's invitation: "Go you
forth and teach all nations"? This call is spoken to
all Christians. Why are so few laymen missionaries?*

*Judging from the missionaries' experience, what are
some principles for forming community? How would
you apply these norms to the communities—city,
neighborhood, parish, school—you live in?*

*What do you think of Father Ferrer's comment on
his job: "We don't want to convert people, to change
their religion. After all, Christian religion is the
religion of love. What we are going there for is to
love people. And this love has to be put into action."*

*"Just the other day I went into an inn for supper,
and there were several men sitting. But there was
one who had nothing to eat. This has struck me.
What was the meaning of that, that a man could
not have a meal? Then I thought that God was absent
from the table of that man and was absent in the
form of bread. And this led me to another consideration, that wherever God is absent from the
table of a man, from the fields of a farmer, then
God is absent also in that form precisely." How is
God absent from your community? How is God
present?*

*"Most of the world is poor, desperately in need of
help." How can we help individually? As a community?*

IN THE FORM OF BREAD

Is there an ultimate meaning to all those things
you have seen just now? Certainly there is an
ultimate meaning.

Just the other day I went into an inn for supper,
and there were several men sitting. But there was
one who had nothing to eat. This has struck me.
What was the meaning of that, that a man could
not have a meal?

Then I thought that God was absent from the
table of that man and was absent in the form of
bread. And this led me to another consideration,
that wherever God is absent from the table of a man,
from the fields of a farmer, then God is absent also
in that form precisely.

Then I saw what was the duty of each of us:
To bring God wherever he is not, in that form in
which he is not present. So my duty was to bring
bread to the table of that man, or to bring water to
the fields, the parched fields of the farmers, or to
bring medicine to the sick. Or to bring consolation
to a man in despair.

Certainly this is the meaning of all our actions.
There is no action which is not divine. Certainly
there is an ultimate meaning to all we have to do.

God is happiness, plenitude, life, abundance.
Where there is no happiness, where there is no
plenitude, where there is no life, then it is my duty
to bring him as I can in the form in which he is not.

That's why you have seen how we bring water
to the fields, how we cure the sick, how we console
the men in desolation. This is the duty of each man,
of a brother to a brother, and whatever things we
do will not only bring bread, bring water, but we
bring God himself in that form of bread and water.

What you have seen has certainly an ultimate
meaning, but it has also an immediate meaning.
And it is this, that we want to build a new India, to
contribute to the greatness of India with our efforts.

We want to help India with dignity. Our
programs are all programs meant to build up not

only men's progress in material things, but also in dignity and respect for his person, because it is when we give ourselves for others that we find a plenitude, the happiness and everything that is in life in us. It is by giving that we get everything, because God gives himself to us.

From script of film "In the Name of God," The Saga of Western Man, *ABC TV, May 20, 1968.*

IN THE NAME OF GOD

John Secondari and Helen Jean Rogers

1968

60 minutes, color or black and white

Purchase: $550.00 color, $312.00 black and white
Rental: $15.00 (ten day loan—black and white)
from Donald Kolson, ABC-TV
7 West 66th Street
New York, N.Y. 10023
(212) LT1-7777

Directed by John Hughs and Walker Stuart
Sound Engineer: Joseph Charman
Cameraman: William Hartigan

THE SOLDIER and
THE LORD IS MY SHEPHERD

The Family Theater has developed an uneven series of films which translate the mood and meaning of different psalms into visual art. The two best films in the series are *The Soldier,* a brilliant rendition of Psalm 41, and *The Lord Is My Shepherd,* Psalm 22.

In *The Soldier,* a soldier is suddenly shot dead while relaxing by a peaceful lake. For several minutes the camera dwells on the single action of the soldier falling, repeating the contour of his fall and capturing the timeless and definitive nature of his death. Psalm 41 is read at the conclusion of the film.

In *The Lord Is My Shepherd* the thoughts of a young schoolboy transform the figures on his school room blackboard into a world of color and animation. Water, flower, and security imagery dominate his imagination. Psalm 22 is read during the film.

Beyond their discussion potential, *The Soldier* and *The Lord Is My Shepherd* have been used successfully at worship services to introduce the service, as sermon aids, and as general visual background at Offertory or Communion time. If played without their sound track, the films provide excellent visual accompaniment to the reading of Scripture. *The Lord Is My Shepherd,* for example, goes well with John 10, 1–19.

The Soldier

What did you see? (After several minutes of brief answers to this question, show the film a second time. Focus on the visual symbols. This might be done without sound.)

What are the symbols saying to you (the sun, shore, sea, bird, offering food, the relation between soldier and bird, the movement upward initially before death)?

Do you think that this film is a good visual prayer? Does it express anything about communication between God and man?

What does Psalm 41 mean? Do the visual symbols deepen one's understanding of God's Word?

Plan how to use this in a Scripture service or the liturgy.

The Lord Is My Shepherd

What did you see? (Show the film a second time. Focus on the symbols.) What did you see the second time?

Did you appreciate more deeply the message of Psalm 22? How is the Lord my shepherd? How does he feed and comfort me? Where does he lead me? Why is the Lord my friend? What are the paths of darkness? What does it mean that the Lord's love and kindness are with me every day of my life?

Plan to use this as part of the Liturgy of the Word during the reading of the Gospel.

Do the psalm films make the meaning of the psalm contemporary? Why? Or why not?

Choose another psalm and make a film or photo-montage of it that contemporizes the meaning.

THE SOLDIER

Family Theater

1966

5 minutes, black and white, 16mm.

Purchase: $25.00 (#19)
Rental: not available

THE LORD IS MY SHEPHERD

Family Theater

1966

5 minutes, black and white, 16mm.

128

Purchase: $25.00 (#19)
Rental: not available

NATIVITY OF JESUS CHRIST

Nativity of Jesus Christ presents nativity scenes from Flemish painters of the fifteenth century. Gospel narration, with a rich background of fifteenth-century music, determines the sequential order of the film. The film's only artistic problem is an overly literal relationship between text and paintings. The Nativity of Jesus Christ would make a good Christmas film for small groups of sensitive students.

Which picture impressed you as being closest to your own image of the nativity?

Did any painting add further meaning to your personal understanding of this event?

Do you react violently against any of these artists' interpretations?

The music is contemporaneous with the Flemish artists. Compare the mood and style of the music with the mood and style of the painting.

Judging from their celebration of Christmas in song and painting, how would you describe the style of faith of the fifteenth-century Flemish Christians?

Create a nativity scene with the mood and style of contemporary music and art that expresses your vision of the birth of Jesus Christ.

What are some of the different traditions of cele-brating Christmas in our country? Compare the

variety of family traditions concerning Christmas within your group.

Related material: refer to DISCOVERY IN SONG, God Is Love, *page 84.*

NATIVITY OF JESUS CHRIST

Religious Films

1958

19 minutes, color, 16mm.

Purchase: inquire (#55)
Rental: $10.00 (#10, #36, #55)

APPENDIX TO LOVE

The Detached Americans
Hutterites
You're No Good
Ask Me, Don't Tell Me
Viva La Calle 103
Window Water Baby Moving
Schmeerguntz
The World of Three

(Related material: For readings on Love confer DISCOVERY IN WORD pp. 59–92)

PEACE

Night and Fog
Time Out of War
Neighbors
The Hole
23 Skidoo
The Hat
Gandhi
A Divided World
Vivre

NIGHT AND FOG

Night and Fog **possesses greater visual and moral impact than any other film discussed in this book and in its field is unequaled by any film in the industry. It presents a picture of German prison camp life during World War II, through which it raises the question of personal responsibility.**

Director Alain Resnais has long been discussing the problem of war in his films. *Last Year in Marienbad, Hiroshima Mon Amour* **and** *La Guerre Est Fini* **all probe the subtleties of human love and freedom against the background of war. In** *Night and Fog,* **Resnais gives his statement the texture of documentary and the dignity of tragedy.**

Color footage of present-day Germany and black and white photography from the actual wartime situation create a dialog between past and present, while pervasive camera motion from left to right communicates a sense of the relentless nature of suffering. The music by Hans Eisler and the commentary by Jean Cayrol achieve a tense counterpoint with the visual by their almost soothing understatement, and the usual pattern of shots within a sequence, from medium to close and close-close-up, situates Resnais' story in an atmosphere of personal exploration. Whether it is the declarative presentation of a shower-room gas-chamber or the terrifying image of a mountain of bodies, piece by piece Resnais builds the memory of a way of life into a warning for the future.

Night and Fog **effectively demonstrates what man at his worst can do to man. It implies that an uncritical value system is criminal.**

Who is responsible? Was the Kapo responsible? Was the soldier?

What role did prejudice against Jews have in permitting and nourishing the Nazi genocide attitude? Did the silent, intelligent German leaders fail in any way?

Is uncritical acceptance of such a criminal value system likely to happen again? Why? Or, why not?

How did Resnais gradually build the impact of the film? What were the most impressive incidents? Why?

Discuss the waste of human potential—what six million dead men could have done. Who are the dead men in today's world? Who is responsible?

For the two years prior to the Arab-Israeli war there were many Nazi-sounding genocidal threats by the Arab leaders. Do you think this caused the Jewish people in the U.S. to recall the German experience?

Compare the movie with Victor Frankl's presentation of his experience as one of the inmates of those horror camps (V. Frankl, Man's Search For Meaning, *Washington Square Press, paper).*

What does Resnais gain by the color-black-white contrast? By his soundtrack? Why does the speed of the camera motion as it moves right, left, or up close remain the same throughout the film?

GENERAL EISENHOWER SPEAKING ABOUT PEACE, IN APRIL 1953

The cost of World War II was 375 billion dollars. With this money it would have been possible to give:
Each family in the Western world including Russia, a $1,000.00 down payment on a home;
Each city with more than a ½ million people

1¼ million dollars for schools and hospitals.

Instead, with this money:
32 million were killed on the battlefields;
20 million—women, old people and children—
were killed in air raids;
23 million people were thrown into concentration camps;
30 million were made cripples;
22 million lost all their possessions;
45 million lost their native land and were
driven to other lands;
30 million dwellings were destroyed;
1 million children lost their parents;
and the spiritual and moral loss and cost . . .

VIETNAM

Vietnam War 1968

How much has the war cost in dollars?
What is the population of Vietnam?
In ten years of war how many have died on battle-
fields?
How many civilians have died in air raids and in
warfare?
In a country where ancestral worship is strong, how
many refugees have been created by the conflict?
How many cities have been destroyed in great part?
How many children have died? How many have
lost their parents?
What is the spiritual and moral loss to the U.S.?

It costs the United States $500,000 to kill one Viet
Cong soldier.
30 billion dollars a year is spent for the war in
Vietnam.
65% of our annual budget ($70 billion) is for
military expenditures. In contrast, the poverty
budget for 1966 was 1.5 billion; foreign aid
amounted to 2.5 billion.

Since 1961 in Vietnam, a country of 15 million
South Vietnamese and 17.3 million North Vietnamese:

over a million civilians were killed.
300,000 military personnel were killed, including more than 25,000 American youth.
4 million have been made refugees—their
homes and villages burned out and destroyed,
5 million gallons of herbicide was used in 1967
to defoliate 150,000 acres of crop-producing
land and 500,000 acres of jungle.
countless maimed and wounded men, women
and children remain without adequate medical care.

NIGHT AND FOG

Como Films and Argos Films
Cocinor, France

1955

31 minutes, color and black and white, 16mm.
Available in French with or without English
subtitles.

Purchase: $250.00 (#17); in Canada (#74)
Rental: $30.00 (#10, #17, #27, #36, #42);
in Canada (#77, #62, #68)

Director: Alain Resnais
Commentary: written by Jean Cayrol
Photography: Ghislain Cloquet and Sacha Vierney
Music: Hans Eisler
The film is based on *Tragedy of Deportations,*
Olgat Wormser
Henri Michael

Awards

Prix Jean Vigo—1965

Scene from *Time Out of War*

A TIME OUT OF WAR

A Time Out of War isolates three soldiers during the Civil War. One Confederate and two Yankee soldiers agree to an hour-long cease-fire. Although separated by a creek, the soldiers trade food and tobacco in weighted handkerchiefs. One Yankee moves upstream to fish while the others exchange small talk and doze. When the hour-long cease-fire is almost over, the Yankee catches a dead Union soldier on his fishing line. The Northerners dig a grave on their side of the creek while the Confederate stands by, silently prolonging their truce. At the conclusion of the film, all three soldiers fire the traditional salute for the dead.

Do you agree with the theme of this film?

How do you think the soldiers felt in this situation?

Did you notice any differences in the Confederate and the Yankee soldiers?

Do you think such a human encounter is possible in war today—e.g., in the Vietnamese War or in the Middle East?

In relation to war, what is the strength and influence on the individual of nationalism and patriotism? Contrast the following attitudes: "My country right or wrong" and the witness of Dietrich Bonhoeffer (cf. D. Bonhoeffer, The Cost of Discipleship, *Macmillan Paper, pages 11–36).*

Look up the facts on the Irish Draft Riots in New York City during the Civil War (cf. E. R. Ellis, The Epic of New York City, *Coward-McCann, 1966, pages 293–317). What caused these riots? How many were killed? What are the dangers to the individual as a person if he is caught up as a cog in the war machinery?*

Eight million died in the Civil War. Was the war necessary to keep the Union? If Lincoln had let the states secede from the Union, would they have returned within ten years? Would the Union be stronger today if it had been retained without war? Which is more effective, economic or military war?

A TIME OUT OF WAR

University of California

1954

22 minutes, black and white, 16mm.

Purchase: $120.00 (#17)
Rental: $10.00 (#10, #17, #27, #36, #42); in Canada (#68)

Producers: Dennis and Terry Sanders
Acting: Barry Atwater, Robert Sherry and Alan Cohen

Awards

Academy Award 1954 (Short Subjects)
Venice Film Festival 1954 (Documentary)
Edinburgh Film Festival
British Film Academy Award
Screen Producers Guild Award 1960
International Festival of Student Films
(Grand Prix Silver Medal—Best Film of the last 10 years)

NEIGHBORS

Neighbors **is about war and a flower. Two neighbors discover that a flower has grown between their homes along their property line. Each neighbor claims the flower for himself and succeeds only in killing his neighbor and destroying the flower. As the film ends, a flower grows from the grave of each neighbor, and the phrase "Love thy neighbor" is flashed across the screen in all the different languages of the world.**

Neighbors **was produced by Norman McLaren who over the years has been recognized as one of Canada's most experimental short filmmakers. Here McLaren works with a jerky, stop-go photographic effect called pictillation and mixes animation and real photography within the same frame.**

Did you feel (*not think*) *any new dimension of the old command: "Love thy neighbor"?*
Why love *your neighbor anyway?*
Is McLaren's answer adequate to the problem he poses? Is it an "answer"?
What effect do the newspaper headlines have on the meaning of the film?
What does the film gain by the use of pictillation?
Christ tells us to love even our enemies, "for what is the merit of loving those who love you?" Is Christ's message possible or practical? If so, how? Would this dilute or strengthen the meaning of love?

Related materials: refer to DISCOVERY IN SONG, Last Night I Had the Strangest Dream, *page 110.*

WHO IS MY NEIGHBOR?

"Master, what must I do to be sure of eternal life?"

"What does the Law say and what has your reading taught you?" said Jesus.

"The Law says, 'Thou shalt love the Lord thy God with all thy heart and with all thy soul and with all thy strength and with all thy mind—and thy neighbor as thyself,' " he replied.

"Quite right," said Jesus. "Do that and you will live."

But the man, wanting to justify himself, continued,

"But who is my 'neighbor' "?

And Jesus gave him the following reply:

"A man was once on his way down from Jerusalem to Jericho. He fell into the hands of bandits who stripped off his clothes, beat him up, and left him half dead. It so happened that a priest was going down that road, and when he saw him he passed by on the other side. A Levite also came on the scene, and when he saw him he too passed by on the other side. But then a Samaritan traveler came along to the place where the man was lying, and at the sight of him he was touched with pity. He went across to him and bandaged his wounds, pouring on oil and wine. Then he put him on his own mule, brought him to an inn and did what he could for him. Next day he took out two silver coins and gave them to the innkeeper with the words: 'Look after him, will you? I will pay you back whatever more you spend, when I come through here on my return.' Which of these three seems to you to have been a neighbor to the bandits' victim?"

"The man who gave him practical sympathy," he replied.

"Then you go and give the same," returned Jesus.

Luke 10, 25–38, from New Testament in Modern English, *trans. J. B. Phillips (Macmillan), pages 159–160.*

NEIGHBORS

National Film Board of Canada

1952

9 minutes, color or black and white, 16mm. and 35mm.
French version released under the title *Voisins*.

Purchase: $100.00 (#17, #34); in Canada $50.00 (#77)
Rental: $5.00 (#10, #17, #27, #36, #42); in Canada (#77, #64, #68)

Production and animated sound by Norman McLaren
Acting by Jean Paul Laudoceur and Grant Munro
Photography by Wolf Koenig
Sound mixing by Clark Daprato

Awards

Award of Merit
Adult Education Section
Third Annual Boston Film Festival 1954
Boston, Massachusetts
Academy Award (Short Film Documentary)
Academy of Motion Pictures Arts and Sciences 1953
Grand Trophy
8th Annual Documentary Film Festival 1955
Salerno, Italy

THE HOLE

Two construction workers peer out of their underground work area and question whether the crane towering above them could ever accidentally drop its cargo on them. Director John Hubley carefully situates their question in the context of possible nuclear warfare.

The Hole is an Academy Award winning animated film. Jazz musician Dizzy Gillespie and George Matthews dub in a brilliant improvised dialog which wanders from household accidents to nuclear warfare. The climax of the film is sudden: a large piece of construction equipment slips from the crane, and at its impact with the ground, Hubley breaks from the level of allegory by substituting an atomic explosion.

"Because it's written it's true." Do you think that what people read in the newspaper is so influential in their lives?

Describe the personalities of the workmen. Was either prejudiced?

"Accidents happen because somebody wants them to happen." Do you agree? Does their analysis of accidents have any legitimate bearing on the problem of war?

What is it to be a citizen of a city? Do you feel you could say "we citizens," accepting the glory and faults of all? Do you think some are forced to be second-rate citizens? Why?

"We run the government, even the lowliest of us. . . ." How significant and creative is this feeling of importance in knowing that he has a part in the government?

Try to relate the story level of the film to the workers' conversation.

"We should scrape all them things (i.e., armaments). . . ." What do you think?

Related materials: refer to DISCOVERY IN SONG, Masters of War, page 118.

Scene from *Neighbors*

WHEN IS WAR NOT AN "ACCIDENT"?

In a statement on world peace the National Conference of Catholic Bishops said:

"While we cannot resolve all the issues involved in the Vietnam conflict, it is clearly our duty to insist that they be kept under constant moral scrutiny. No one is free to evade his personal responsibility by leaving it entirely to others to make moral judgments. . . .

Americans can have confidence in the sincerity of their leaders as long as they work for a just peace in Vietnam. Their efforts to find a solution to the present impasse are well known. We realize that citizens of all faiths and of differing political loyalties honestly differ among themselves over the moral issues involved in this tragic conflict. While we do not claim to be able to resolve these issues authoritatively, in the light of the facts as they are known to us, it is reasonable to argue that our presence in Vietnam is justified. . . . But we cannot stop here. While we can conscientiously support the position of our country in the present circumstances, it is the duty of everyone to search for other alternatives. And everyone—government officials and citizens alike—must be prepared to change our course whenever a change in circumstances warrants it. . . .

On the basis of our knowledge and understanding of the current situation, we are also bound always to make sure that our government does, in fact, pursue every possibility which offers even the slightest hope of a peaceful settlement. And we must clearly protest whenever there is a danger that the conflict will be escalated beyond morally acceptable limits. . . .

There is a grave danger that the circumstances of the present war in Vietnam may, in time, diminish our moral sensitivity to its evils. Every means at our disposal, therefore, must be used to create a climate of peace. . . . In the spirit of Christ, the Christian must be the persistent seeker in the Gospel, the man willing to walk the second mile. He walks prudently, but he walks generously and he asks that all men do the same."

(*taken from J. O'Gara,* The Church and War, *pages 57–58*)

WHEN IS IT A "JUST" WAR?

The Christian may involve himself in war by way of exception. It must be a "just war." The "just war" doctrine is not a license for certain wars, but rather a list of minimal criteria without which any war is certainly unjust. These requirements which have to do with a war's basic causes, the motives of the men and nations engaged in it and the means by which it is prosecuted include the following:

The war must be the *last resort* after all peaceful means of solving the conflict have been exhausted;

The war must be an act of *defense* against *unjust* demands backed by *aggressive* force;

The war must be declared by the legally constituted authority of the nation concerned;

There must be a reasonable possibility of victory;

The harm caused by the war must not outweigh the good hoped for; and

The military tactics and objectives of the war must discriminate between soldiers and civilians.

(*from* Ave Maria, *May 27, 1967, page 11*)

Scene from *The Hole*

THE HOLE

Storybord, Inc.

1962

15 minutes, color, 16mm., animated

Purchase: $195.00 (#8, #50); in Canada (#68)
Rental: $10.00 (#8, #27, #36)

Director: John Hubley
Animation: Gorg Mooney and Bill Littlejohn
Improvised Dialog: Dizzy Gillespie, George
Matthews

Awards

American Film Festival Blue Ribbon Award—1964
Academy Award—1963
Venice Film Festival Grand Prize—1963

23 SKIDOO

23 Skidoo is a photographic essay about a city after a neutron bomb explosion. A neutron bomb destroys only living cells, leaving everything else undamaged. 23 Skidoo communicates a depressing absence of life and implies that the value of human life ought not to be subordinated to the value of military victory.

23 Skidoo makes its point with silence and picture-perfect "empty" shots. A city without life means a silent train waiting to go; it means milk bottles left standing in a doorway, an empty escalator moving quietly without people, and blown paper on a silent street. Whenever sound is introduced in the film, it serves only to intensify the silence, as, for example, the echoes of a choir in an empty church and concert music played to empty seats.

Because of its visual excellence, 23 Skidoo achieves a mood adequate to its question and should stimulate an interested discussion about the relative value of human life.

How did the linking of picture and sound contribute to the impact?

Is there any progression or contrast in the selection of images through which the director speaks?

How do you react to the final image—the whirlpool of worthless papers?

What is the meaning of the title 23 Skidoo? Do you think such a possibility as presented in this movie is realistic?

How should one form an opinion on the value of the "bomb"? Is it a moral question? How do you feel about America using the "bomb"?

Would you agree that the film is saying more— something like: "War is a neutron bomb; war kills the soul even if it lets people move, function and prosper as before"?

Related materials: refer to DISCOVERY IN SONG, What Have They Done to the Rain?, page 115.

THE CHRISTIAN AND WAR

Our faith must be dominated by the thought of peace. The Christian conscience must always try harder and harder to draw stricter limits to the permissibility of war. Christians must try to implement such statements as those of Pope John in Pacem in terris: "Hence justice, common sense and

Scene from *23 Skidoo*

a sense of human dignity demand urgently that the competition in armaments should cease, that the offensive weapons at the disposal of each country should be everywhere and simultaneously reduced, that the atomic weapons should be forbidden, and that, finally, all countries should agree to simultaneous disarmament with mutual and effective inspection."

The total atomic war is an evil of unknown magnitude compared to other wars. The question of the lawfulness even of defensive armaments with atomic bombs must be answered, at least by a passionate effort to make such weapons effectively—that is, on both sides—non-existent. . . .

The sober considerations of scientists, who speak the same language all over the world, will perhaps play a role in the establishment of mutual confidence, which, as *Pacem in terris* says, is the one real basis of peace. But the prophetic passion of those whose eyes have been opened to the madness of war, and who are properly organized to prevent it, will be indispensable in alerting our consciences more and more thoroughly. The conscientious refusal of military service should be possible. As the council says, "Furthermore, proper provision should be made in law for those who refuse military service for reasons of conscience. Another form of service to the community may be envisaged in such cases" (*Church in the World,* no. 79). The council, however, does not make this obligatory; it leaves it to the individual judgment. Hence it also has a word to say to those who work for peace while carrying out military duties: "Those who serve their country in the armed forces must also regard themselves as guardians of the security and freedom of their country, and contribute, by the proper fulfillment of their military service, to a real and stable peace" (*Church in the World,* no. 79). The council has special praise for statesmen who work for peace: "We must support the efforts of the many men of

good will who, in spite of the burdens of high office, feel it their serious duty to strive for the outlawing of war, which they abhor, though they cannot alter the complications of the actual situation" (*Church in the World,* no. 82).

from A New Catechism (*Herder and Herder*), *pages 424–425.*

23 SKIDOO

National Film Board of Canada

1964

8 minutes, black and white, 16mm.

Purchase: $50.00 (#18); in Canada $33.00 (#77) Rental: $6.00 (#34, #42); in Canada (#64, #68, #77)

Producer and Director: Julian Briggs Photographer: Paul Leach

Awards

Diploma of Merit, Crakow, Poland—1965 1st Prize, Salerno Festival of Short Films—1965 Nominee—U.N. Award—1965 Nominee—Best Short Film—British Film Awards—1965

THE HAT

The Hat **is much like** *The Hole* **and was produced with the same Academy Award winning team of John Hubley on production and Dizzy Gillespie on dialog.** *The Hat,* **filmed two years after** *The Hole,* **studies the same problem of military disarmament. A soldier on border patrol accidentally**

Scene from *The Hat*

drops his hat across the boundary line into enemy territory. The soldier and his enemy counterpart must decide what to do. Is shooting the answer? By reducing the problem to the absurd level of a hat, the film makes its point clearly.

The tall soldier says that "war as a means of settling disputes is obsolete." Do you agree? Is war obsolete because of the discovery of "the bomb"?

"It's evolution, mate. . . . We have to adapt ourselves." What are the new conditions in modern life to which man must adapt himself? Do you think man is capable of adapting to fit these new conditions?

"What's the first thing you do to do away with war? —Disarm!" Do you think this is reasonable? If so, what should be the conditions of disarmament? Why?

"We must have some kind of authority." Because world peace is a world problem, would you be willing to delegate to a world authority the necessary power to maintain peace? What powers should such a world authority need to keep the peace? Do you think we have taken any steps in this direction?

How are fear and suspicion generated in one nation against another? Can you suggest ways of combating such fear and suspicion both on a national and on a personal level?

"Why don't you step over on my side. You might like it." Do you think our national programs of cultural exchange, getting to know the other fellow, help to avoid war? Why? Or, why not?

Related materials: refer to DISCOVERY IN SONG, The Universal Soldier, page 117.

THE ARMS RACE

Men should be convinced that the arms race in which so many countries are engaged is not a safe way to preserve a steady peace. Nor is the so-called balance resulting from this race a sure and authentic peace. Rather than being eliminated thereby, the causes of war threaten to grow gradually stronger.

While extravagant sums are being spent for the furnishing of ever new weapons, an adequate remedy cannot be provided for the multiple miseries afflicting the whole modern world. Disagreements between nations are not really and radically healed. On the contrary, other parts of the world are infected with them. New approaches initiated by reformed attitudes must be adopted to remove this trap and to restore genuine peace by emancipating the world from its crushing anxiety.

Therefore, it must be said again: the arms race is an utterly treacherous trap for humanity, and one which injures the poor to an intolerable degree. It is much to be feared that if this race persists, it will eventually spawn all the lethal ruin whose path it is now making ready.

(from Constitution on the Church in the Modern World *par. 81 in* Documents of Vatican II *ed. W. Abbott, S.J.)*

THE HAT

Sterling Educational Films
Under auspices of World Law Fund

1964

18 minutes, color, 16mm., animated

Purchase: $220.00 (#28); in Canada (#74)
Rental: $15.00 (#10, #27, #36, #42); in Canada (#70)

Producers: John and Faith Hubley
Subject Impromation: Dizzy Gillespie, Rudley Moore

Awards

First Prize for Best Cartoon, Venice Film Festival
and Tours Film Festival—1964
Special Medal Award of the Independent Motion
Picture Distributors and Exhibitors Society—1964

GANDHI

"Self-discipline is more powerful than the military weapons of rulers."

Mohandas Karamehand Gandhi and Rev. Martin Luther King, Jr. were prophets of non-violence and men who identified themselves with the poor. Gandhi was murdered in 1948; Martin Luther King was slain immediately before Passion Week in 1968, twenty years after Gandhi and twenty centuries after Christ, the model for both of them. For Gandhi and King, their answer of love to violence involved a risk, their vulnerability. Yet the answer of violence, if apparently safer, seemed to them shallow and ultimately futile. Violence could never allow their suppressed people to respond with freedom and productivity. Love could. But the significance of Gandhi must be related not simply to Martin Luther King and Jesus Christ; his context is the entire dialog between violence and non-violence in man's history: the passive suffering of the Christian martyrs under the Roman emperors as opposed to the belligerent Christian spirit during the Crusades; the bloody revolutions, French, American, and Russian, contrasted with the Indian revolution; and the neutral position of Switzerland in World War II contrasted with our own.

Gandhi had three great campaigns in his life: the liberation of India from British domination; the liberation of India from religious and caste disunity; and the liberation of the poor, his Harijans or children of God, as he called them, from their misery. In 1930, against the British, Gandhi undertook his famous salt march to the sea. The purpose of the march was to manufacture salt in violation of British law. At that time, thousands of Gandhi's followers were arrested for infractions of various laws. In 1932 Gandhi began a fast unto death because of the threatened political separation of the untouchable caste from the rest of Indian society. The fast succeeded, and to his death in 1948 Gandhi fasted on countless other occasions in his attempt to bring unity to the Hindu-Moslem rift within his people.

Gandhi is photographed in traditional documentary style. It incorporates footage and stills from the historic situations themselves and is well organized. *Gandhi* succeeds as a film because the story it tells is of heroic stature and because its message is pertinent to us today.

What kind of man was this Mohandas Gandhi, the prophet of non-violence? How is he relevant to our life?

From his life what do you see as the main principles of his non-violent philosophy?

Would you say that Gandhi was a success? Why?

Gandhi felt very deeply that in the midst of death life persists, and that in the midst of untruth truth persists, and that in the midst of darkness light persists. He looked at his world and opted for life, truth and light. How do you feel about your world? What do you search for?

To violence he brought the forceful strength of non-

violence. To hatred he returned love and desire for brotherhood. How would you express similar attitudes in your world?

How did Martin Luther King put into effect Gandhi's principles of non-violence? Does the United States government act in relation to the race problem in any way like the British government in India during Gandhi's struggle?

Related materials: refer to DISCOVERY IN SONG, I Ain't Marchin' Anymore, *page 120.*

RELIGION OF NON-VIOLENCE

Non-violence in its dynamic condition means conscious suffering. It does not mean meek submission to the will of the evil-doer, but it means the putting of one's whole soul against the will of the tyrant. Working under this law of our being, it is possible for a single individual to defy the whole might of an unjust empire, to save his honor, his religion, his soul, and lay the foundation for that empire's fall or its regeneration.

And so I am not pleading for India to practice non-violence because she is weak. I want her to practice non-violence being conscious of her strength and power. No training in arms is required for a realization of her strength. We seem to need it, because we seem to think that we are but a lump of flesh. I want India to recognize that she has a soul that cannot perish and that can rise triumphant above every physical weakness and defy the physical combination of a whole world. What is the meaning of Rama, a mere human being, with his host of monkeys, pitting himself against the insolent strength of ten-headed Ravan surrounded in supposed safety by the raging waters on all sides of Lanka? Does it not mean the conquest of physical

might by spiritual strength? However, being a practical man, I do not wait till India recognizes the practicability of the spiritual life in the political world. India considers herself to be powerless and paralyzed before the machine guns, the tanks and the airplanes of the English. And she takes up non-cooperation out of her weakness. It must still serve the same purpose, namely, to bring her delivery from the crushing weight of British injustice, if a sufficient number of people practice it.

Mohandas K. Gandhi, "Young India," in The Pacifist Conscience, *P. Mayer, Aug. 1920 (Regnery), page 218.*

PHILOSOPHY OF NON-VIOLENCE

[These are] the basic aspects of this philosophy:

First, it must be emphasized that non-violent resistance is not a method for cowards; it does resist. If one uses this method because he is afraid or merely because he lacks the instruments of violence, he is not truly non-violent. This is why Gandhi often said that if cowardice is the only alternative to violence, it is better to fight. He made this statement conscious of the fact that there is always another alternative: no individual or group need submit to any wrong, nor need they use violence to right the wrong; there is the way of non-violent resistance. This is ultimately the way of the strong man. It is not a method of stagnant passivity. The phrase "passive resistance" often gives the false impression that this is a sort of "do-nothing method" in which the resister quickly and passively accepts evil. But nothing is further from the truth. For while the non-violent resister is passive in the sense that he is not physically aggressive toward his opponent, his mind and emotions are always active, constantly seeking to persuade his opponent that he is wrong. This method is passive physically, but strongly active spiritually. It is not passive non-resistance to evil; it is active non-violent resistance to evil.

A second basic fact that characterizes non-violence is that it does not seek to defeat or humiliate the opponent but to win his friendship and understanding. . . . The aftermath of non-violence is the creation of the beloved community, while the aftermath of violence is tragic bitterness.

A third characteristic of this method is that the attack is directed against the forces of evil rather than against persons who happen to be doing the evil. It is evil that the non-violent resister seeks to defeat not the persons victimized by evil. . . . The tension is, at bottom, between justice and injustice, between the forces of light and the forces of darkness. And if there is a victory, it will be a victory not merely for fifty thousand Negroes, but a victory for justice and the forces of light. We are out to defeat injustice and not white persons who may be unjust.

A fourth point that characterizes non-violent resistance is a willingness to accept suffering without retaliation, to accept blows from the opponent without striking back. "Rivers of blood may have to flow before we gain our freedom, but it must be our blood," Gandhi said to his countrymen. . . . "Things of fundamental importance to people are not secured by reason alone, but have to be purchased with their suffering. Suffering is infinitely more powerful than the law of the jungle for converting the opponent and opening his ears which are otherwise shut to the voice of reason."

A fifth point concerning non-violent resistance is that it avoids not only external physical violence but also internal violence of spirit. The non-violent resister not only refuses to shoot his opponent but he also refuses to hate him. At the center of non-violence stands the principle of love. The non-violent resister would contend that in the struggle for human dignity, the oppressed people of the world must not succumb to the temptation of becoming bitter or indulging in hate campaigns. To retaliate in kind would do nothing but intensify the existence of hate in the universe. Along the way of life, someone must have sense enough and morality enough to cut off the chain of hate. This can only be done by projecting the ethic of love to the center of our lives.

In speaking of love at this point, we are not referring to some sentimental or affectionate emotion. It would be nonsense to urge men to love their oppressors in an affectionate sense. Love in this connection means understanding, redemptive good will.

A sixth basic fact about non-violent resistance is that it is based on the conviction that the universe is on the side of justice. Consequently, the believer in non-violence has deep faith in the future. This faith is another reason why the non-violent resister can accept suffering without retaliation. For he knows that in his struggle for justice he has cosmic companionship. It is true that there are devout believers in non-violence who find it difficult to believe in a personal God. But even these persons believe in the existence of some creative force that works for universal wholeness. Whether we call it an unconscious matchless power or infinite love, there is a creative force in this universe that works to bring the disconnected aspects of reality into a harmonious whole.

Abridged from pp. 101–106 in Stride Toward Freedom (*hard bound ed.*) *by Martin Luther King Jr. Copyright 1958 by Martin Luther King Jr. Reprinted by permission of Harper & Row, Publishers*

COMMITMENT CARD
FOR NON-VIOLENT VOLUNTEERS:

I hereby pledge myself—my person and body—to the non-violent movement. Therefore I will keep the following ten commandments:

1. MEDITATE daily on the teachings and life of Jesus.

2. REMEMBER always that the non-violent movement in Birmingham seeks justice and reconciliation—not victory.

3. WALK and TALK in the manner of love, for God is love.

4. PRAY daily to be used by God in order that all men might be free.

5. SACRIFICE personal wishes in order that all men might be free.

6. OBSERVE with both friend and foe the ordinary rules of courtesy.

7. SEEK to perform regular service for others and for the world.

8. REFRAIN from the violence of fist, tongue or heart.

9. STRIVE to be in good spiritual and bodily health.

10. FOLLOW the directions of the movement and of the captain of a demonstration.

I sign this pledge, having seriously considered what I do and with the determination and will to persevere.

From pp. 61–62 in Why We Can't Wait *(hard bound ed.) by Martin Luther King Jr. Copyright 1963 by Martin Luther King Jr. Reprinted by permission of Harper & Row, Publishers*

GANDHI

Wolper Productions

1964

26 minutes, black and white, 16mm.

Purchase: $150.00 (#28); in Canada (#74)
Rental: $7.50 (#36, #42, #28)

A DIVIDED WORLD

Survival is a harsh reality of the animal world which fosters clear divisions of strength and fear. *A Divided World* **is primarily about the animal world, yet the symbolic and photographic sensitivity of Arne Sucksdorff, one of the film industry's most brilliant cameramen, raises questions about man's own divided world and his future in evolution.**

A Divided World **opens with a shot of a gaseous swamp. It is winter. A small animal sniffs cautiously near his burrow, senses danger and hides. A fox pursues and kills a rabbit. An owl then defeats the fox for possession of the dead rabbit. The film concludes with a shot of a snug and warmly lit cabin. The story is simple, and there is no vocal soundtrack; Sucksdorff combines natural noises, silence and Bach's** *Fantasia.*

Most audiences find *A Divided World* **puzzling. The story, although simple, is at first difficult to piece together, perhaps because of Sucksdorff's unusual photography. The audience effort to deal with the puzzling and the symbolic, however, inevitably leads to a greater perception of theme. Is there a statement of evolution in** *A Divided World*? **What are the norms for division within the animal world? At the end of the film, is Sucksdorff pointing to civilization with a question?**

How did the naked loneliness and cold atmosphere affect you?

What are the dimensions of division expressed in this film?

As the film opens, smoke is coming up from the swamp; as it ends, smoke is rising from the chimney of the house. Do you see any relation in this?

One hunts the other, but they are all really hunters. One kills another in order to survive. This is frequently physically true in the animal world. Is there a parallel on the human physical level? On the emotional level of human activity? On the social level of human activity?

Search out photographs, paintings or songs that describe the divided world of men. Is it merely "natural" that men are divided? Should we stop dreaming and accept a clear law of nature? Or is there some sound reason for thinking and feeling differently about our own divided world?

A DIVIDED WORLD

Arnie Sucksdorff
Janus Films

1961

10 minutes, black and white, 16mm.

Purchase: $75.00 (#26); in Canada (#63)
Rental: inquire (#26, #36)

VIVRE

To Live **interprets life in our world through a series of images related to war and death. The film is composed of authentic newsreel material issued over the past twenty years and edited in the style of contemporary cinema. Shots of death by firing squad, prisoners of war, refugees, a bombed city and other wartime situations appear in rapid succes-** **sion and question the meaning of life. The film-maker asks the audience directly to consider whether events similar to those reported in the film are taking place somewhere in the world today.**

What were your feelings as you watched these news-reels of the past twenty years? What kinds of people did you see?

What were your reactions as you watched the prisoners delivered, numbered and questioned? How did you feel as you watched refugees leaving home, women and children going to prison camps? As you saw the lonely children, their mothers and the old people?

What questions or reflections did these feelings arouse?

The filmmaker states very simply: "Similar scenes are taking place somewhere in the world. . . ." Where?

What is the significance of the title?

Was the director's technique of clipping old news films effective? If so, why? If not, why not?

Related materials: refer to DISCOVERY IN SONG, Blowin' in the Wind, *page 123.*

VIVRE

Carlos Vildardebo

1959

8 minutes, black and white, 16mm.

Purchase: $75.00 (#12)
Rental: $7.50 (#17)

APPENDIX TO PEACE

The House
21-87
World in a Marsh
Overture
Time of the Locust
The Soldier

(*Related material: For readings on Peace confer*
DISCOVERY IN WORD pp. 114–136)

HAPPINESS

An Occurrence at Owl Creek Bridge
Runner
Very Nice, Very Nice
Chartres Cathedral
Sacrifice and Resurrection
String Bean
My Own Back Yard To Play In
21-87
Roadsigns on a Merry-Go-Round
Automania 2000
World in a Marsh
Prehistoric Images
The House

AN OCCURRENCE AT OWL CREEK BRIDGE

An Occurrence at Owl Creek Bridge **essentially follows the short story of the same name by Ambrose Bierce. However, Robert Enrico, the director of the film, emphasizes, with greater depth than Bierce, the theme of time in conflict with man's desire to live.**

Man wishes so intensely to cling to life that the moment of death is said to become psychologically long enough for the memories of a lifetime. In *An Occurrence at Owl Creek Bridge,* **a Civil War prisoner faces death by hanging. The prisoner projects his escape in fantasy during the split second required to carry out his execution. Only at the end of the film, when the prisoner hangs lifeless, does the viewer realize that death, not life, has been victorious. A twig floating gently downstream, a watchcase snapped shut, and the lingering memory of home confronted with the inevitable and final pull of rope establish the paradox of fresh awareness of life at the moment of its passing. In** *An Occurrence at Owl Creek Bridge,* **Enrico has formulated for his audience an element of their own situation—life growing through time toward death.**

How does Enrico communicate a desire for life in this film? What symbols, shots and elements in the sound track help him?

Does the sound distortion in the shooting sequence achieve its effect or is it too self-conscious?

How does Enrico use time in his film? Toward the end of the film, there is a sequence where the main character meets his wife. Do you feel that there is a flaw in this sequence? Why could Enrico have possibly left it out?

At times the hard wooden bridge or the delicate spider's web conveys a sense of texture. How can a photograph communicate a sense of texture? Is this done frequently in the film? Does Enrico relate it to theme?

What is the final comment on life made by the film?

How does the written story by Ambrose Bierce differ from the film?

LIFE IS

Life is wearing buttons.
Life is being cool.
Life is conformity to ———— (parents, peers, girl/boyfriend, Church, boss).
Life is groovy.
Life is communicating to persons.
Life is feeling high.
Life is experience.
Life is action.
Life is doing your thing.
Life is a happening now, not a hope.
Life is living for others.
Life is what I see and touch, what is present to the sensible proportion of my intellect.
Life is mystery.
Life is a process of becoming.
Life is a becoming free.
Life is love.
Life is a manner of living: a life of hope, a life of poverty, a life of love.
Life is growing young—to appraise life honestly, with experience, not naively, but critically with openness and sensitivity.

AN OCCURRENCE AT OWL CREEK BRIDGE

The Film was originally produced in France by
Marcel Ichac and Pauk de Roubaix, 1962

1962

27 minutes, black and white, 16mm.

Purchase: $200.00 (#17); in Canada (#74)
Rental: $17.50 (#10, #17, #27, #36); in
Canada (#71, #64, #68)

Director: Robert Enrico
Adapted from Short Story by Ambrose Bierce

Awards

Academy Award Winner, 1964
(Best live action short subject)
Cannes Festival Winner, 1962—Grand Prize

RUNNER

Runner **is a beautifully photographed essay
about the art of running. The film observes the
style of Bruce Kidd, a track star who runs one
hundred miles every week. W. H. Auden wrote
and narrates the sound track which is slightly
pretentious although effective in raising the general
question intended by the filmmaker: What does it
mean to practice the art of running, and what kind
of person does it involve?**
Everything about *Runner* **implies nobility.
Hours of dedication, precision training, endurance,
loneliness and little public appreciation are all
elements of a runner's life emphasized in the film.**
Runner **presents a perfect opportunity to discuss
the value of athletics with regard to its effect on the
individual, school and community. Every viewing
audience will have members who have participated
in team sports and who will enjoy sharing their
experiences.**

Interpret this film as a visual parable.

*What do you think were the feelings of Bruce Kidd
as he raced?*

*What are the qualities of good sportsmanship? Explain these in terms of popular baseball, football,
track, hockey and basketball players.*

How does a person develop these qualities?

Are sports in fact enjoyed even by the losers?

*What do you think is the place of sports in the
growth of the person? What is more important in
the young person's growing up—his sports' program
or his academic life? Why?*

*What is the relation between athletics and growing
up socially? What place in a school program should
sports take?*

THE REALM OF SPORT

For me, Williams is the classic ballplayer of the
game on a hot August weekday, before a small
crowd, when the only thing at stake is the tissue-
thin difference between a thing done well and a
thing done ill. Baseball is a game of the long season,
of relentless and gradual averaging-out. Irrelevance—
since the reference point of most individual games
is remote and statistical—always threatens its interest, which can be maintained not by the occasional
heroics that sportswriters feed upon, but by players
who always care; who care, that is to say, about

Scene from *Runner*

themselves and their art. Insofar as the clutch hitter is not a sportswriter's myth, he is a vulgarity, like a writer who writes only for money. It may be that, compared to managers' dreams such as Joe DiMaggio and the always helpful Stan Musial, Williams is an icy star. But of all team sports, baseball, with its graceful intermittences of action, its immense and tranquil field sparsely settled with poised men in white, its dispassionate mathematics, seems to me best suited to accommodate, and be ornamented by, a loner. No other player visible to my generation has concentrated within himself so much of the sport's poignance, has so assiduously refined his natural skills, has so constantly brought to the plate that intensity of competence that crowds the throat with joy.

The afternoon grew so glowering that in the sixth inning the arc lights were turned on—always a wan sight in the daytime, like the burning headlights of a funeral procession. Aided by the gloom, Fisher was slicing through the Sox rookies, and Williams did not come up to bat in the seventh. He was second up in the eighth. This was almost certainly his last time to come to the plate in Fenway Park, and instead of merely cheering, as we had at his three previous appearances, we stood, all of us—stood and applauded. Have you ever heard applause in a ball park? Just applause—no calling, no whistling, just an ocean of handclaps, minute after minute, burst after burst, crowding and running together in continuous succession like the pushes of surf at the edge of the sand. It was a somber and considered tumult. There was not a boo in it. It seemed to renew itself out of a shifting set of memories as the kid, the Marine, the veteran of feuds and failures and injuries, the friend of children, and the enduring old pro evolved down the bright tunnel of twenty-one summers toward this moment. At last, the umpire signaled for Fisher to pitch;

with the other players, he had been frozen in position. Only Williams had moved during the ovation, switching his bat impatiently, ignoring everything except his cherished task. Fisher wound up, and the applause sank into a hush.

Understand that we were a crowd of rational people. We knew that a home run cannot be produced at will; the right pitch must be perfectly met and luck must ride with the ball. Three innings before, we had seen a brave effort fail. The air was soggy; the season was exhausted. Nevertheless, there will always lurk, around a corner in a pocket of our knowledge of the odds, an indefensible hope, and this was one of the times, which you now and then find in sports, when a density of expectation hangs in the air and plucks an event out of the future.

Fisher, after his unsettling wait, was wide with the first pitch. He put the second one over, and Williams swung mightily and missed. The crowd grunted, seeing that classic swing, so long and smooth and quick, exposed, naked in its failure. Fisher threw the third time, Williams swung again, and there it was. The ball climbed on a diagonal line into the vast volume of air over center field. From my angle, behind third base, the ball seemed less an object in flight than the tip of a towering, motionless construct, like the Eiffel Tower or the Tappan Zee Bridge. It was in the books while it was still in the sky. Brandt ran back to the deepest corner of the outfield grass; the ball descended beyond his reach and struck in the crotch where the bullpen met the wall, bounced chunkily, and, as far as I could see, vanished.

Like a feather caught in a vortex, Williams ran around the square of bases at the center of our beseeching screaming. He ran as he always ran out home runs—hurriedly, unsmiling, head down, as if our praise were a storm of rain to get out of. He didn't tip his cap. Though we thumped, wept, and chanted, "We want Ted," for minutes after he hid in the dugout, he did not come back. Our noise for some seconds passed beyond excitement into a kind of immense open anguish, a wailing, a cry to be saved. But immortality is non-transferable. The papers said that the other players, and even the umpires on the field, begged him to come out and acknowledge us in some way, but he never had and he did not now. Gods do not answer letters.

From "Hub Fans Bid Kid Adieu," by John Updike, The Realm of Sport, *ed. H. W. Wind (Simon and Schuster, 1966), pages 66 and 70–71.*

RUNNER

National Film Board of Canada

1962

12 minutes, black and white, 16mm.

Purchase: $50.00 (#17, #34); in Canada $33.00 (#77)
Rental: $5.00 (#10, #17, #34, #42); in Canada (#77, #64, #68)

Producer: Tom Daly
Director and Script: Donald Owen
Commentary: W. H. Auden
Music: Don Douglas
Photographers: John Spolton
　　　　　　　　Greg Borremous

Awards

Honorable Mention
Film as Art
International Film Festival 1963–64
San Francisco, California

VERY NICE, VERY NICE

Very Nice, Very Nice **is a complicated representation of American society by means of rapid, cumulative close-up and quick-cut shots. People, objects and events rush together in a style of pop-art distortion. The result is an atmosphere of estrangement, impersonalism and materialism, the standard problems and accusations associated with American society. The sound track contributes to this atmosphere by snatches of conversation which indicate the frequent contradictions between American theory and action. At the conclusion of the film, the narrator claps his hands as if in a concert hall and remarks, "Very nice, very nice," his final comment on our society's ability to cope with its world.**

What are the characteristics of American society presented in this film? Are they reducible to a single, coherent pattern? *Very Nice, Very Nice* **is a stimulating discussion film because its multiple images make it impossible for the audience to agree about any single interpretation of the film. Perhaps a second screening after several minutes of discussion would be enlightening.**

Answer in 3 ways (first to come to mind): What have you just seen? How do you feel about seeing what you just saw? What one shot do you recall most clearly? What one statement do you recall most sharply?

Can you connect statements with pictures? What pictures are shown as a voice is saying: "Almost everybody has a washing machine, a dryer. . . ." Were there any sequences that seemed united by a single theme?

A man says: "There's no real concern. . . . People

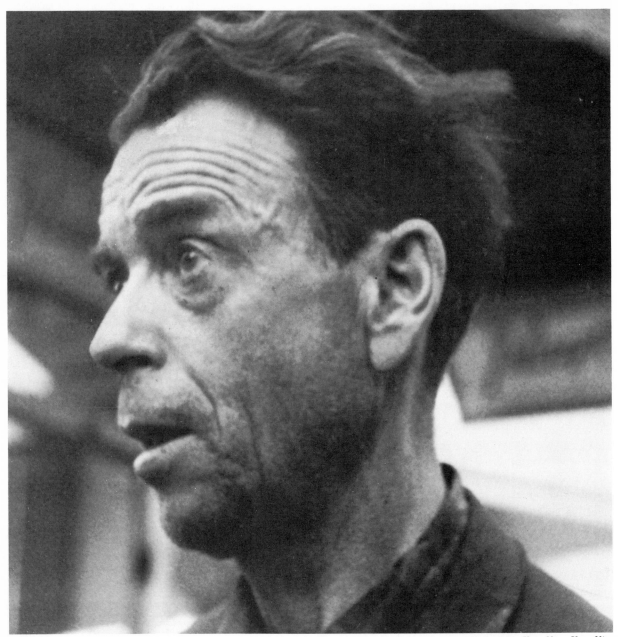

Scene from *Very Nice, Very Nice*

seem unwilling to become involved." What does the director say in his visual comment on this statement?

The apocalyptic rally sequence with its Savanarola-like preacher terminates in three questions: "What is the meaning of life? What is good? What is a value?" Does this film mirror the meaning of American life, i.e., society's values, its pace and its future goals?

"Warmth and brightness will return and renew all the hopes of men." Should you try to escape to an island of warmth, or should you attempt to change the situation? How would you plan a renewal of hopes?

How effective is the director in using angle shots and collages and relating the sound track to his images?

After a second screening of the film, did your impression of its meaning change?

Related material: refer to DISCOVERY IN SONG, Satisfaction, page 91.

VERY NICE, VERY NICE

National Film Board of Canada

1961

8 minutes, black and white, 16mm.

Purchase: $90.00 (#34, #17); in Canada $17.00 (#77)
Rental: $10.00 (#10, #17, #27); in Canada (#77, #64, #68)

Director: Arthur Lipsit

Awards

Nominee—Best Live Action Film
Academy of Motion Picture Arts and Sciences
Special Prize—Tours Film Festival—1962
Chris Certificate Award—Columbus Film Festival—1962

CHARTRES CATHEDRAL

Chartres Cathedral **is a picture-perfect display film about Chartres Cathedral and is narrated by John Canaday, art critic of the** *New York Times* **and editor of the Metropolitan Museum of Art series** *Metropolitan Seminars in Art.* **The cathedral itself, in the words of Canaday, is one of the most daring structures created by man. But more than a curiosity of engineering, the cathedral represents a model of life in the Middle Ages. The spires of Chartres symbolized for medieval man an elevation of spirit from material burdens, while its stained glass and sculpture were the only Bible available to the illiterate majority. If for modern man knowledge explains mystery, for medieval man all knowledge led to mystery. Chartres Cathedral was for him a medieval encyclopedia, with all knowledge visibly organized and pointing toward the mystery of God. Even the cathedral's use of light and space and the logic of its engineering, with its thrust and counterthrust, created a sense of mystery and became a symbol for God.**

Chartres Cathedral **is a film of value for students of art, history or religion and presents an opportunity for team teaching in these areas.**

THE SACRIFICE AND THE RESURRECTION

The Sacrifice and the Resurrection **charts the seven-year architectural history of Coventry Cathedral which was completed in 1962. The film is an unprecedented record in the history of cathedrals because never before has a cathedral been constructed in a single lifetime.** *The Sacrifice and the Resurrection* **is more than an historical document, however, for it carefully explicates the relationship between the contemporary architecture of Coventry and contemporary philosophic and religious values. It presents the rationale for major decisions made by the architect and artists and craftsmen who built the cathedral, while it shows these men and their work in progress.**

Coventry Cathedral itself is a complicated product resulting from the work of a worldwide community of men, and it is truly an example of the relation between contemporary symbol and contemporary meaning. From these points of view and many others, Coventry Cathedral compares superbly with any other cathedral in history. If shown in sequence with *Chartres Cathedral, The Sacrifice and the Resurrection* **presents an immediate dramatization of man's evolution as manifest in architecture.**

Chartres is a symbol of medieval man, a symbol of his integrating faith, intellect and engineering, all blending to effect mystery—the symbol of God. How is Coventry a symbol of modern man?

Chartres communicates the feeling of mystery and thought process of medieval man. What do the symbols of modern man say about his meaning and feelings? How do the modern artists portray modern man?

Can a person lose his sense of mystery by being too scientific?

Today, how are faith and learning related? How are faith and learning integrated into action?

How did Chartres contribute to establishing a relevant Christian community? How has the reality of a meaningful Christian community evolved between Chartres and Coventry? Is this evolution a growth or decline in community? What is the future of relevant Christian community?

Contrast Coventry Cathedral to a Gothic cathedral. How does this reflect a change in the people who built the two cathedrals?

Is it possible to introduce a contemporary spirit into religious ritual? How?

Discuss the effect of time on the building of Coventry Cathedral.

Recall the major pieces of art that particularly impressed you (cf. below). What justifies them as meaningful and appropriate religious work?

Chartres Cathedral
1. *Bas-relief over doors*
2. *Statues of saints on columns*
3. *Use of stained glass*
4. *Altar and general interior*

Coventry Cathedral
1. *Stations of the Cross*
2. *Statue of St. Michael*
3. *Use of glass: abstract baptistry window, etched glass of entrance-way, transparent chapel glass*
4. *Altar and general interior*

CHARTRES CATHEDRAL

Encyclopaedia Brittanica Films

1962

30 minutes, color, 16mm.

Purchase: $360.00 (#18); in Canada (#66)
Rental: $17.50 (#36, #42, #61); $6.00
in Canada (#68)

Narrator: John Canaday
Director: John Barnes

THE SACRIFICE AND THE RESURRECTION

Charles Laing, Limited

1963

40 minutes, color, 16mm.

Purchase: Must be bought in England
Rental: $12.00

Executive Council of Episcopal Church
815 2nd Avenue
New York, N.Y. 10017
212 TN 7-8400

STRING BEAN

An old Parisian seamstress plants a single bean seed in a flower pot by her window. She demonstrates toward it a tenderness and care which is habitual to her and yet remembered from another time. Her actions imply both hope and sadness. The seamstress is old, and her hours are spent in slow performance of the routine actions necessary to maintain life. She putters dutifully about her single room, obtains water from a hallway faucet,

cooks, sews and cares for her bean plant. When the plant has reached a certain maturity, the seamstress sits quietly with it in the Luxembourg Gardens, near her home, furtively unwrapping it from her handbag so that it may grow well in the sunlight. One day the seamstress realizes that the plant is too large for her flower pot. She transplants it and leaves it in the public gardens. The park caretakers soon uproot the plant and discard it with the weeds. The woman hurries by their workplace and takes the mature beans from her plant. As the film concludes, she carefully plants three string bean seeds in her flower pot.

String Bean combines color footage with black and white. This technique emphasizes the distinction between flowering life and the single-room existence of the old seamstress. The implications of the film arise both from its story line and this technique. What is old age? What are the conditions of its existence? Is its relationship to life only that of memory and hope?

Would you like to be like this woman when you grow old? Why? Or, why not?

Walk slowly up the stairs as the old woman had to. In what ways is an elderly person limited?

What do you think were the feelings of this old person? Were they similar to Eleanor Rigby's? To Pope John XXIII's? What does being old mean to you?

Did her actions and personality give hints of what she was like as a young woman?

Do you think she was happy? Why? Or, why not?

Why did she plant the string bean seeds once again at the end of the film?

What do you think the director was saying by his contrasting black and white with color footage?

Did sharing this old woman's experience have any relevance to your life?

Related material: refer to DISCOVERY IN SONG, The Flower Lady, pages 30–31, and Eleanor Rigby, pages 64–65.

STRING BEAN

Originally produced in France

1964

17 minutes, black and white and color, 16mm.

Purchase: $175.00 (#17); in Canada (#74)
Rental: $15.00 (#17, #27, #36, #42)

Producer: Claudon Capar
Director: Edmon Sechan

Awards

Golden Palm Award, Cannes Film Festival

MY OWN BACK YARD TO PLAY IN

To city children there is magic in a ten-cent rubber ball, an empty alleyway or an old tire. Kid-chant and a jump rope open worlds of possibility to children whose scenery is primarily pavement and wall. "We pretend that the street is water and we go back and forth on it." The interior imagination as expressed in children's street games can be as beautiful as the more formal play of supervised playgrounds.

My Own Back Yard To Play In shows this positive aspect of city children's life, and yet, as the film develops, there is a strange sense that their happiness is perhaps too greatly make-believe. "I just pretend. I don't know what to think about." At the conclusion of the film, several children are asked what they would like to become when they grow up. Some are children's wishes: "I'd like to be a cowboy." "I"d like to take Mickey Mantle's place." Others are more serious and want to be doctors or teachers. One child, however, reveals the harsh reality ultimately implied by the entire film: "I want my own yard to play in . . . my own back yard to play in . . . my own back yard to play in."

How much influence do you think the atmosphere and sounds of the streets have on the children?

What are the sounds and scenes of your neighborhood? What influence do they have on your life?

What hopes of the children are revealed in the game "what I want to be and do"? How does your own environment influence your aspirations?

Did you ever pretend the street was water? Do you remember reading fairy tales? Do you see any value in "fairy tale" pretending—either in reading or acting out?

Does your "own back yard" include your school? Your church? Your home?

Are you tuned in to the poetry of sight and sound of your own block? What makes up the poetry of your neighborhood?

KID-CHANT

It's raining, it's pouring, the old man is snoring.
Bumped his head and he went to bed and he
    couldn't get up in the morning.

Rain, rain, go away
Come again some other day.

Starlight, star bright,
First star I see tonight,
Wish I may, wish I might,
Have the wish I wish tonight.

Ladybug, ladybug, fly away home
Your house is on fire and your children will burn.

Well, I won't be my father's Jack,
And I won't be my mother's Jill.
But I will be a fiddler's wife and fiddle
Where I will.

Ready or not, here I come.

Heavy, heavy hangs over thy head.
What must the owner do to redeem it?

One potato, two potato, three potato, four.
Five potato, six potato, seven potato more.

Down the Mississippi, by the muddy Mississippi
Where the boats go *push*.

London Bridge is falling down, falling down, falling
    down.
London Bridge is falling down, my fair lady.

MY OWN BACK YARD TO PLAY IN

Edward Harrison

1959

7 minutes, black and white, 16mm.

Purchase: $110.00 (#17); in Canada (#68)
Rental: $5.00 (#10, #17, #36, #42); in Canada
(#68)

Producers and Editors: Pat Jaffe, Larry Silk,
John Schulyz, and Peggy Lawson
Director and Photographer: Phil Lerner
Sound: Tony Schwartz
Sound Track: *City Sounds,* Folksways Record
C-7341 (Tony Schwartz)

Awards

First Prize, Social Subject, Venice Film Festival
First Prize, Oberhausen Film Festival

21-87

21-87 **develops the theme of dehumanization through a series of images loosely related to isolation and loneliness. The film is confusing at times. There is no story line, and frequently the images rushing at the viewer seem contradictory in their effect. The grotesque image of a person in flames is included in the film as is a beautifully photographed tree in sunlight. The viewer is never certain whether the film is simply disorganized or trying to convey a complicated state of consciousness and failing—or succeeding. Nevertheless, the rapid series of strangely angled shots, the occasional distortion of speed within the film, and a sound track with enigmatic clips of conversation make** *21-87* **an exciting film open to many interpretations.**

Did you see or feel any theme develop in this film?

What was the setting at the beginning of the film? What mood did the skull and the clown and the atomic explosion produce? Did you read any meaning in these images?

Relate the sound track to the visual. What images were shown during the following:

> *"I have found something even more satisfying . . ."*
> *"I don't believe in immortality . . ."*
> *"You're 21-87."*
> *"[The] body of our Lord Jesus Christ was given to preserve you till life everlasting."*

Recall the images contemplating nature. Did you ever wonder at the mysteries of the sun and sky and flowers and life? Did you see any meaning?

Do you think the director related the city to the circus? If so, why?

What do you think is the meaning of the title 21-87?

THE UNKNOWN CITIZEN

(To JS/07/M/378 This Marble Monument Is Erected by the State)

He was found by the Bureau of Statistics to be
One against whom there was no official complaint,
And all the reports on his conduct agree
That, in the modern sense of an old-fashioned word,
    he was a saint,
For in everything he did he served the Greater
    Community.
Except for the War till the day he retired
He worked in a factory and never got fired,
But satisfied his employers, Fudge Motors Inc.
Yet he wasn't a scab or odd in his views,
For his Union reports that he paid his dues,
(Our report on his Union shows it was sound)
And our Social Psychology workers found
That he was popular with his mates and liked a drink.

The Press are convinced that he bought a paper
    every day
And that his reactions to advertisements were normal
    in every way.
Policies taken out in his name prove that he was
    fully insured,
And his Health-card shows he was once in hospital
    but left it cured.
Both Producers Research and High-Grade Living
    declare
He was fully sensible to the advantages of the
    Installment Plan
And had everything necessary to the Modern Man,
A phonograph, a radio, a car and a frigidaire.
Our researchers into Public Opinion are content
That he held the proper opinions for the time of year;
When there was peace, he was for peace; when there
    was war, he went.
He was married and added five children to the
    population,
Which our Eugenist says was the right number for
    a parent of his generation,
And our teachers report that he never interfered with
    their education.
Was he free? Was he happy? The question is absurd:
Had anything been wrong, we should certainly have
    heard.

—W. H. Auden

Mr. Auden has recorded "The Unknown Citizen" (LP, Library of Congress, PL 21).

From Collected Shorter Poems 1927–1957 *by W. H. Auden. Copyright 1940 and renewed 1968 by W. H. Auden. Reprinted by permission of Random House Inc. and Faber and Faber Limited*

21-87

National Film Board of Canada

1963

10 minutes, black and white, 16mm.

Purchase: $90.00 (#7, #34); in Canada $33.00 (#77)
Rental: $5.00 (#7); in Canada (#77, #68, #64)

Director: Arthur Lipsit

ROADSIGNS ON A MERRY-GO-ROUND

Martin Buber, Dietrich Bonhoeffer and Pierre Teilhard de Chardin have formulated a new awareness of individual human dignity and Christian optimism in the face of the impersonalism, genocide and agnosticism that they discovered in modern society. *Roadsigns on a Merry-Go-Round* **is a photographic essay of unusual quality interpreting the narrated thought of these three thinkers. It is a film for thoughtful audiences and a catalyst for those students beginning the style of poetic questioning for which Buber, Bonhoeffer and Teilhard de Chardin have been so well remembered. Because of its difficulty,** *Roadsigns on a Merry-Go-Round* **is worth discussing in three segments.**

"I am a believer, a passionate believer! I have a terrible fear of not believing. Not believing is like not existing." What do you believe in? What have you passionately set your heart on?

What are the roadsigns expressing the mood and character of our society? Of today's young adult society?

How does one become and grow as an "honest, straightforward man"?

Give examples of what Buber means by:

"Without It *man cannot live. With* It *alone man is not a man."*
"Through Thou *a man becomes* I. *Only then can an* I-It *relationship be established."*

How can we transfer God "from the plane of the imaginary to the plane of the real"?

Does Christianity stand for restraint of passion?

How do we find God and accept him in the ways he comes?

How do we learn to live with our own contradictions, with our own doubts?

"What am I to do? You shall not withhold yourself." Is this true?

What can we do to "make the crowd no longer a crowd"?

Related material: refer to DISCOVERY IN SONG, Crucifixion, pages 80–83.

ROADSIGNS

They sit in their automobile while the indifference of nature sets their pensive mood for them. With childhood reminiscence of escape and fantasy finished, the anxious need for love cured, and survivalist perils surmounted in the secular grace of modern luxury, they know that for them, the quest for fulfillment has only begun. They have affirmed in their wedlock that there is a life worth living, but burning in them is the realization that "there is something about living that demands believing." What is it? Belief in what? They want to help each other live through the ideological dark in which they still

Scene from *Road Signs on a Merry-Go-Round*

reside, but "how much does anyone know of belief?" All men are out on the same limb of unbelief alongside each other, and all they can do is "check the frontiers together to see if there be any new signs of faith."

Bonhoeffer saw man as a creature who has spent his long history discovering the inadequacy of his own rationalism. Rationalism leads to fanaticism; fanaticism makes duty the absolute; and duty eliminates that sense of moral responsibility in which evil must be opposed. Man at his finest is not obedient man but what he called the "honest, straightforward man." Chardin held man to be the "evolutionary axis" of the world, the one in whom evolution becomes so "conscious of itself" that man will of necessity "form one body and soul in an orderly charity." We must, therefore, trust in "the growing unity of man's ability and potential." He envisioned a "new coming humanity."

Buber, to me, is the most interesting and profound of the three men. At the base of all his philosophy is the concept of the I-Thou encounter. Man is supreme because in him dialogue and relationship can be fully realized. He contends that our lives are constantly being addressed from without. We must establish dialogue with these voices in terms of a relationship in which one makes the correspondent a "Thou" and not an "It." At birth we are released from a captive "I-Thou" in the womb and take on the "I-It" of nature. Then, in this world of "I-It," we live by our "instinct to give relationship to the universe." That is, we reach out for the indefinite "Thous," for only through a "Thou" can a man become truly "I," truly himself. Once he has redeemed his own universe in an "I-Thou" relationship, he sees it all more microscopically and luminously.

Why is this adventure attributed to a man and a woman? How can they be by themselves the persons who stand before the vast repositories of thought which these men of the mind have given us? How can they speak to them in ways that represent what the vast majority of faith-seekers today feel inside? They can because they appropriately give a kind of iridescent form to what is perhaps the major aspect of synthesis between the three thinkers. One could call it an ontological implication of sex. Bonhoeffer, with his vision of a twentieth century in which man is no longer capable of being religious, subsumed the love of earthly affection under one's proverbial need of loving God with the whole heart. And he especially saw in the passionate intercourse between a man and a woman an expression of that outreach for the God who is in and of his world. Chardin saw lovers coming into the greatest possession of themselves when they can affirm that they are "lost in each other," and this quality of union should be seen growing and expanding until it embraces all the earth, namely, the being of God himself. Buber has found in the twofold nature of man and woman the very twofold nature of existence, the most dramatic example of the I-Thou encounter, which in turn makes contact with the one great Love.

R. Racine, Mass Media Ministries *(May, 1968)*

HYMN TO MATTER

'Blessed be you, harsh matter, barren soil, stubborn rock: you who yield only to violence, you who force us to work if we would eat.

'Blessed be you, perilous matter, violent sea, untameable passion: you who unless we fetter you will devour us.

'Blessed be you, mighty matter, irresistible march of evolution, reality ever new-born; you who, by constantly shattering our mental categories, force us to go ever further and further in our pursuit of the truth.

'Blessed be you, universal matter, immeasurable time, boundless ether, triple abyss of stars and atoms and generations: you who by overflowing and dissolving our narrow standards of measurement reveal to us the dimensions of God.

'Blessed be you, impenetrable matter: you who, interposed between our minds and the world of essences, cause us to languish with the desire to pierce through the seamless veil of phenomena.

'Blessed be you, mortal matter: you who one day will undergo the process of dissolution within us and will thereby take us forcibly into the very heart of that which exists.

'Without you, without your onslaughts, without your uprootings of us, we should remain all our lives inert, stagnant, puerile, ignorant both of ourselves and of God. You who batter us and then dress our wounds, you who resist us and yield to us, you who wreck and build, you who shackle and liberate, the sap of our souls, the hand of God, the flesh of Christ: it is you, matter, that I bless.

'I bless you, matter, and you I acclaim: not as the pontiffs of science or the moralizing preachers depict you, debased, disfigured—a mass of brute forces and base appetites—but as you reveal yourself to me today, *in your totality and your true nature.*

'You I acclaim as the inexhaustible potentiality for existence and transformation wherein the predestined substance germinates and grows.

'I acclaim you as the universal power which brings together and unites, through which the multitudinous monads are bound together and in which they all converge on the way of the spirit.

'I acclaim you as the melodious fountain of water whence spring the souls of men and as the limpid crystal whereof is fashioned the new Jerusalem.

'I acclaim you as the divine *milieu,* charged with creative power, as the ocean stirred by the Spirit, as the clay moulded and infused with life by the incarnate Word.

'Sometimes, thinking they are responding to your irresistible appeal, men will hurl themselves for love of you into the exterior abyss of selfish pleasure-seeking: they are deceived by a reflection or by an echo.

'This I now understand.

'If we are ever to reach you, matter, we must, having first established contact with the totality of all that lives and moves here below, come little by little to feel that the individual shapes of all we have laid hold on are melting away in our hands, until finally we are at grips with the *single essence* of all subsistencies and all unions.

'If we are ever to possess you, having taken you rapturously in our arms, we must then go on to sublimate you through sorrow.

'Your realm comprises those serene heights where saints think to avoid you—but where your flesh is so transparent and so agile as to be no longer distinguishable from spirit.

'Raise me up then, matter, to those heights, through struggle and separation and death; raise me up until, at long last, it becomes possible for me in perfect chastity to embrace the universe.'

Down below on the desert sands, now tranquil again, someone was weeping and calling out: 'My Father, my Father! What wild wind can this be that has borne him away?'

And on the ground there lay a cloak.

From Hymn of the Universe *by Pierre Teilhard de Chardin. Copyright © 1961 by Editions du Seuil. Copyright 1965 in the English Translation by William Collins Sons & Co. Ltd., London, and Harper & Row, Publishers, Inc., New York*

ROADSIGNS ON A MERRY-GO-ROUND

Columbia Broadcasting System, Inc.

1967

60 minutes, color, black and white, 16 mm.

Purchase: color $550.00; black and white $275.00 (#12)
Rental: $25.00 (#27); in Canada (#75)

Marvin Silbersher

AUTOMANIA 2000

Notes from a Diary, January 1, 2000:

Man has achieved a society for worldwide affluence, an inexhaustible flow of consumer goods, freedom from all want, and even liberation from the bother of cooking. One problem remains, however. The population has been confined to automobiles for the past five years. In fact, car-dwellers cannot remember the time when it was possible to actually move in cars. Car is piled on top of car, forming a solid wall, a skyscraper of autos complete with drivers and families. Those on the lower levels of these rapidly growing car walls must rely exclusively on auto-television for their impressions of the outside world. In the face of this universal immobility, war has become unthinkable, and science has devoted itself to supplying the needs of car-dwellers. Top-level living now means the newest and highest automobile, while science, once again keeping pace with progress, has developed its final invention, an auto-producing automobile.

What do you think the director of this film is saying?

Do you think such chaos is possible? Or is it totally imaginative? Explain your reasons.

What is the rate of car production in the United States? Is this good or bad for American growth?

How does the film measure progress? How would you measure the progress of society?

Could the evolution of the car and world traffic congestion be symbols of other elements in our society?

Describe a similar film that would portray the future wonders of automation.

THE DYNAMIC WORLD OF CHANGE

Writing on "The Era of Radical Change" in *Fortune* magazine, Max Ways has said, "Within a decade or two it will be generally understood that the main challenge to U.S. society will turn not around the production of goods but around the difficulties and opportunities involved in a world of accelerating change and ever-widening choices. Change has always been a part of the human condition. What is different now is the pace of change, and the prospect that it will come faster and faster, affecting every part of life, including personal values, morality and religions, which seem most remote from technology. So swift is the acceleration that trying to make sense of change will come to be our basic industry. Aesthetic and ethical values will be evolving along with the choices to which they will be applied. The question about progress will be 'how good?' rather than 'how much?' "

He goes on to point out that "the break between the period of rapid change and that of radical change is not sharp; 1950 is an arbitrary starting

Scene from *Automania 2000*

date. More aspects of life change faster until it is no longer appropriate to think of society as mainly fixed, or changing slowly, while the tide flows around it. So many patterns of life are being modified that it is no longer useful to organize discussion or debate mainly around the relation of the new to the old. The movement is so swift, so wide and the prospect of acceleration so great that an imaginative leap into the future cannot find a point of rest, a still picture of social order."

We are told that 25 percent of all the people who ever lived are alive today; that 90 percent of all the scientists who ever lived are living now; the amount of technical information available doubles every ten years; throughout the world, about 100,000 journals are published in more than 60 languages, and the number doubles every 15 years.

We are told these things, but we do not always act as if we believed them. "The fact is," says Alvin Toffl in *Horizon* in the summer of 1965, "—and simple observation of one's own friends and associates will confirm it—that even the most educated people today operate on the assumption that that society is relatively static. At best they attempt to plan by making simple straight-line projections of present trends. The result is unreadiness to meet the future when it arrives. In short, 'future shock.' "

From D. Fabun, The Dynamics of Change *(Prentice-Hall), pages 4–5.*

AUTOMANIA 2000

Halas and Batchelor Studios

1963

10 minutes, color, 16mm. animated

Purchase: $125.00 (#17); in Canada (#74)

Rental: $12.00 (#17, #27, #61); in Canada (#64)

Producer: John Halas

Awards

Moscow International Film Festival 1963
Silver Prize (Best Cartoon)
Locarno International Film Festival (Best Animated Film)
Barcelona International Film Festival (Best Animated Film)

WORLD IN A MARSH

World in a Marsh **presents the life habits, battles and reproductive processes of marsh creatures. The marsh is a world without mercy. Its curious hierarchy of swamp bug, water nymph, bullfrog, snake and heron is based on the harsh rules of survival. Although ten to one hundred thousand eggs are produced by a single female frog, the frog population of the marsh remains relatively static. The red wing feeds its young mainly with dragonfly eggs. It requires one hundred neut eggs to produce a single pair of neuts for the following year.**

World in a Marsh **is a beautifully photographed film, but its undisguised presentation of marsh life gradually awakens the awareness, unstated directly in the film, that human life is in some way related to the totally natural and non-rational process of survival in the marsh world. The nature of this relationship is central to any notion of man as rational and as individual and is perhaps the most important topic of discussion suggested by the film.**

How is man *subject to this evolutionary process of survival? Yet man rises above this mere survival. In what ways does he control his environment and*

the processes of nature which form him?

In light of the above, what is a person's responsibility for this process? How does the value of human life fit in? What does this mean about man's future? ·

Why or why not would genocide be a natural manifestation of the processes of survival? What about gene regulation?

CHRIST, THE EVOLVER

In this connection we may say of Teilhard what Père Benoit says of St. Paul: The essential thing in his eyes, what he really had at heart, was "to maintain the absolute primacy of Christ," and Teilhard's preoccupation with stars that may possibly be inhabited is an apposite reminder, *mutatis mutandis,* of Paul's preoccupation with the angelic powers in the epistle to the Colossians. Occasionally, one can note a slip in Teilhard's wording, but in his thought we find the very opposite of any "Minimism." We can see, too, that all Père Teilhard's Christology is for him the living bond between prayer and action. It is from the very heart of his mystical life that springs the apostolic flame with which he is afire. "The majority of men who learn to read nowadays learn that Christ is a thing of the past." That judgment is taken from a recent book. In some intellectual circles such expressions as "post-Christian thought," "post-Christian culture," "the post-Christian era," are freely used. Père Teilhard had noticed this with distress. But he did not lose heart. He did not "seek in the heavens some other star than Christ." Following the example of St. Paul in his mission to the Gentiles of the first century, Teilhard—the modest but eager disciple of the great Apostle—sought to preach Christ, the same Christ,

to the dechristianized Gentiles of his own day. Instead of taking refuge in some illusory figure greater than Christ, he cried, "O Christ, ever greater!"

In the shape of a "little one" in his mother's arms—in harmony with the great law of birth— You have taken root in my infant soul, Jesus. And now, repeating and extending in me the circle of Your growth in the Church—now that the humanity You put on in Palestine has gradually spread to all parts, like a halo of countless colors, in which Your Presence penetrated every other presence around me, superanimating it, never destroying. . . .

The more the years pass, my Lord, the more I seem to know that, in me and around me, the great, hidden, care of modern Man is much less to quarrel over possession of the World than to find some way to escape it. The anguish of feeling not spatially but ontologically imprisoned in the cosmic Bubble! The anxious search for an outcome—no, a focus—for evolution! There—the price we have to pay for a still-growing planetary inflooding—is the grief that, dimly discerned though it be, weighs heavy on the mind of Christian as of Gentile, in this world of today.

Beyond and above itself, Humanity, now emerged into consciousness of the movement that draws it along, has ever increasing need of some Direction, some Solution, to which at last it can give its allegiance.

And so—this God, no longer only the God of the old cosmos, but the God of the new cosmogenesis (precisely inasmuch as the effect of a mystical work, now two thousand years old, is to show us in You, beneath the Child at Bethlehem and the Crucified, the Beginning and the collective Kernel of the World itself)—this God, so longed for by our generation —is it not You, You, indeed who are this God— and You who bring him to us—Jesus?

Lord of Consistence and Union, You whose distinguishing mark and essence are that You can grow indefinitely, without distortion or break, in time with the mysterious Matter at whose heart You lie and of all whose movements You are the final controller—Lord of my childhood and of my end —*God, fulfilled for Himself, and yet for us, God whose birth has no end*—God who, since You offer Yourself for our adoration as "evolver and evolutive," are now the only God who can bring us satisfaction—tear away at last all the clouds that still veil You—and tear away the clouds, too, of hostile prejudices and false beliefs.

And grant that in diaphany and in flame, Your universal presence may spring forth.

O Christ, ever greater!

From Teilhard de Chardin: the Man & His Meaning *by H. de Lubac. Copyright © 1965 by Burns & Oates, Ltd. Published by Hawthorn Books, Inc. 70 Fifth Avenue, New York, New York*

WORLD IN A MARSH

National Film Board of Canada

1955

22 minutes, color and black and white, 16mm.

Purchase: $250.00 (#28, #34); in Canada $120.00 (#77)
Rental: $8.50 (#28, #61); in Canada (#77, #68, #64)

Producer and Director: David Bairstow
Photography: William Carrick
Film Editor: Maureen Balfe
Musical Score: Robert Fleming

Awards

Blue Ribbon
American Film Festival 1961
New York, New York

1st Award

National Science Category, 1957
Padua, Italy

1st Prize
Scientific Films 1957
Rapallo, Italy

PREHISTORIC IMAGES

Prehistoric Images **tours the Lascaux caves in France where Stone Age man has left a painted record of his life. The Lascaux paintings were completed ten to forty thousand years ago and are considered to be among the first records of intelligent life. The artist has left us a colorful array of prehistoric animals and in many ways has identified himself. He was capable of perspective and rational design, as the interlocked hoofs of two bulls and a series of patterned cow heads indicate. A number of grid-like signs perhaps demonstrate his ability to write in some primitive symbolic language. Was this Stone Age artist fully man? How fully are his paintings a representation of life?** *Prehistoric Images* **is worth discussing in the context of evolution.**

What do you think the artist of Lascaux was trying to say in his paintings?

Do you think that the paintings could have had any religious significance?

How has art evolved since the Lascaux cave painting? How has the artist evolved?

Why does man paint images? Must he so express himself?

What would be the images of modern man to be found in the caves in the future?

PREHISTORIC IMAGES

Brandon Films

1955

17 minutes, color, 16mm.

Purchase: $250.00 (#8)
Rental: $17.50 (#8, #36, #42)

Director: Thomas L. Rowe Arcady

Awards

Certificate of Excellence
International Art Film Festival
New York, 1957

THE HOUSE

The House is the history of a large family home built in Belgium at the turn of the century and torn down after World War II. The storyline of *The House* is scattered in non-linear fashion throughout the film, effecting a sense of event which is fragmented and at the same time unified by the dominant image of the house itself. It is almost as if the house were remembering in the haphazard way that humans remember, present and past mixed together and forming a complex consciousness transcending time. "In my end is my beginning." The viewer feels that every moment of the history of the house is suffused through every other moment.

Once untangled, the plot of *The House* reads very simply. A young gentleman decides to build a house for himself and his bride. The architect of the house and the gentleman's bride fall in love. She gives birth to a daughter who grows and marries. During World War II, German troops occupy the house and shoot the daughter's husband. The house is eventually torn down by wreckers.

In the film as it actually is, shots of the destruction of the house alternate with shots of its construction; shots of its vivid success contrast with shots of its ruin. And on the human level, the strangely combined events of birth and death repeat what the film technique already implies about the life of the house: birth and death, comedy and tragedy, the contrasting moments of linear time, have in fact a fundamental unity, the duration or experience of the individual.

The House should generate many levels of discussion. Does life have greater significance than that of a repeatable pattern? What does time mean, and how does it relate to the experience of the individual? Exactly how does the unusual film technique contribute to the thematic level of the film? Is anything implied about the significance of our 20th century?

Trace the storyline of The House. *Who are the characters? What is the connotation of the stuffed animals and the forest? What is the role of the soldiers?*

Does the repeated scene of the house being torn down have significance?

Why do you think the opening and last scenes were almost identical? Compare visual and verbal metaphor.

In your life what events stand out as significant, as formative of you?

In the history of your city, what events gave a character or personality to the community?

What is time that it can be so distorted?

Scene from *The House*

MYSTERY OF TIME

I said just now that we measure time as it passes, and in such a way that we are able to say that one period of time is twice as great as another, or of the same length, and so on of any other parts of time which are measurable. For this reason, as I said, we measure time as it is passing, and if I am asked how I know this, I should reply that I know it because we do measure time, and we cannot measure what does not exist, and the past and the future do not exist. But do we measure the present, since it has no extent? It is measured while it is passing; when it has passed by it is not measured, for then there will be nothing there to measure.

But where does time come from, by what way does it pass and where is it going to when we are measuring it? It can only come from the future, it can only pass by way of the present, and it can only go into the past. Therefore, it comes from something which is not yet in existence, it passes through something which has no extension, and it goes in the direction of something which has ceased to exist.

But how can we measure time except in some sort of extension? When we say single and double and triple and all the other expressions of this sort which we use about time, we must be speaking of extensions or spaces of time. In what kind of extension, then, do we measure time as it is passing by? In the future, from which it comes? But we cannot measure something which is not yet in existence. In the present, through which it passes? But we cannot measure something which has no extension. In the past, toward which it is going? But we cannot measure something which no longer exists.

From The Confessions of Saint Augustine, *translated by Rex Warner. Copyright © 1963 by Rex Warner. Reprinted by permission of The New American Library, Inc., New York*

THE HOUSE

Louis Van Gasteren
Originally produced in the Netherlands

1961

32 minutes, black and white, 16mm.

Purchase: $250.00 (#17); in Canada (#74)
Rental: $30.00 (#17); in Canada (#68)

Writers: Louis Van Gasteren and Jan Vrigman
Photographer: Eduard van der Enden
Music: Else van Epen

Awards

Award, International Federation of Film Societies, 1961
Golden Gate Award, San Francisco Film Festival, 1961
Edinburgh Film Festival, 1961
Berlin Film Festival, 1961
Cork Film Festival, 1961
Arnhem Film Festival, 1961

APPENDIX TO HAPPINESS

Two Men and a Wardrobe
Sky
Leaf
Nativity of Jesus Christ
The Hand
The Detached Americans
Hutterites
Interview With Bruce Gordon
The Lord Is My Shepherd
In the Name of God

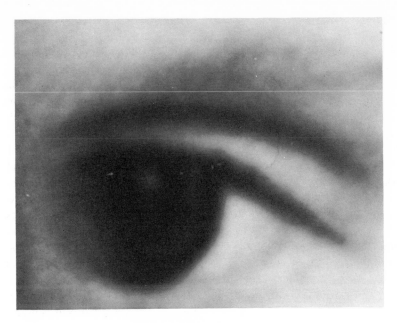

THE UNDERGROUND

Not As Yet Decided
Dodge City
Happy Birthday, Felisa
Requiem
Window Water Baby Moving
Thanatopsis
Time of the Locust
Schmeerguntz
Sampler (of Warhol)
Science Friction

No definition of underground filmmaking is completely valid, yet in general it can be said that the underground encompasses a wide variety of people who make low budget films for what they suspect will be a limited circulation. They have something to say and believe that the moving image is the way to say it, although they differ widely in their manner of speaking. In fact, individuality is perhaps the most generic quality of underground filmmaking. Underground filmmakers experiment both in film technique and meaning; frequently they consider images and subject matter not ordinarily dealt with in public media. With its anti-war, anti-convention and anti-film film, the underground frequently becomes a harsh critic of society, and there is a definite sense of liberation from censorship associated with this criticism. But pervasive to all underground filmmaking is a mission of new awakening. The underground filmmaker seems to be saying: See images as if for the first time. Recognize your situation as if for the first time. See how you are trapped. See also how beautiful life really is.

For detailed information about the underground film cf. An Introduction To The American Underground Film *by Sheldon Renan (Dutton Paperback: New York, 1967).*

JEFF DELL

In keeping with the highly personal nature of the underground, this in-depth critique of Jeff Dell is included. Jeff Dell is a 32-year-old New Yorker who calls his film company Anifilm Studios. He is the proud father of two children and often worries about their future. It is his habit in his films to confront their innocence with the violence and injustice of the world they are growing into. *Not As Yet Decided,* Dell's earliest film, is a photographic essay contrasting footage of his own children with still shots of racial unrest—dogs on a leash, a Black Power rally, men wearing gas masks—all photographed in the North.

Dell was asked by the New Line Cinema newsletter if *Dodge City,* his second film and a statement against war, had any political overtones. He replied, "If you mean is it also 'anti-Vietnam,' the answer is no, not particularly. War pictures are the same from whatever conflict they're taken. But I am a father, the father of one of the kids in the film, in fact. Right now they're innocent, and soon they'll have enough of the problems they have created for themselves to face. I'm frightened for them. Today there is too much that is too ominous—too much just out of control." In *Dodge City* Dell punctuates a children's game with photography from the two world wars, the Spanish Civil War and the Korean and Vietnam wars.

In *Happy Birthday, Felisa,* Dell combines a birthday party for Felisa Ann Dell with scenes of unrest and violence—for example, the Florence floods, the ghetto riots, the Texas tower gunman and Vietnam. Dell's integration of color with black and white achieves a brilliant family home-movie vs. newsreel contrast. Parents' talk at the children's party, the lighting of cigarettes and the eating of ice cream and cake become the background for fire and murder and starvation. *Requiem,* Dell's most recent film, is a film essay in memory of Dr. Martin Luther King, Jr.

Jeff Dell, like many of the underground filmmakers, is anxious to communicate personally with his viewers. He reluctantly quoted rental prices for his films, stating that he would much prefer to have interested parties call him directly.

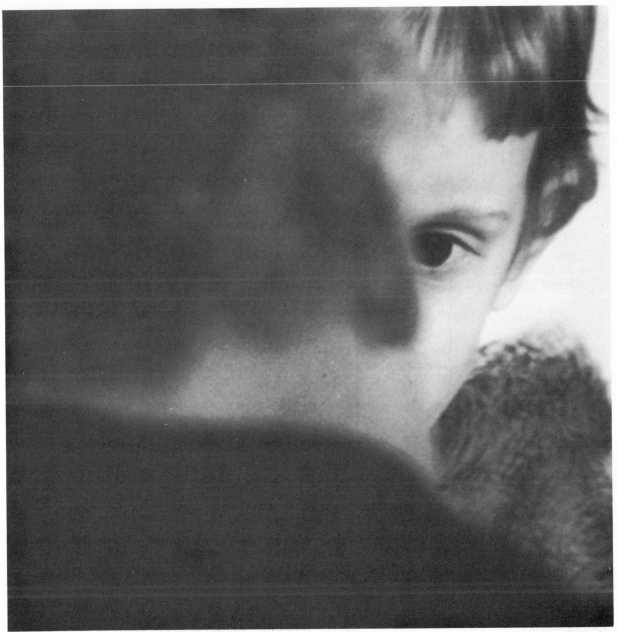

Scene from *Dodge City*

HAPPY BIRTHDAY, FELISA

*What do you feel Jeff Dell was saying as you shared
Felisa's birthday party?*

*How do the parents' conversation, the events of
today's world and the children at the party relate to
or reveal one another?*

Do you think that Dell forces the issue?

*What do the parents mean by "culturally deprived"
and "black militancy"? What meaning do these
terms have to the deprived and the militants? What
do they mean to you?*

*What are the sources of violence in our world? What
are examples of violence in your own world?*

*Does Dell's integration of color and black and white
footage succeed?*

*Jeff Dell gives a world-view of our day. Present a
collage of your own world-view of today.*

INTERVIEW WITH JEFF DELL

Q.

Jeff, how would you describe underground
filmmaking?

A.

Well, it's a form of expression, you know. And
I think that most of the people doing underground
films really want to say something and they don't
have the money to really do a good finished product.
But the things that come out of it—some of the
things are really worthwhile.
And all of them have some quality. Nothing is
really garbage.

Now in a sense I'd rather not be considered an
underground filmmaker. I'd rather be thought of as a
professional filmmaker. But if I have to be
classified as an underground filmmaker because of
the type of films I produce, then I'm an underground
filmmaker.

Q.

Well, why do you produce your kind of film?

A.

Why? Because I have something to say. And to
do something for people, you know, with all the
killing.

Q.

How do your films help?

A.

I hope they're making people see the meaningless-
ness of hating each other—to maybe understand
a little more about war and civil rights or whatever
the film is about.
They're not comedies.
Now, I haven't got a solution.
I think things are being done, like civil rights, but
I haven't got a solution.
Who has?
I think it's important that people should make films
with messages like this even though there's no
solution—because it's a way of presenting a problem
without killing someone.
You can take a gun and kill the things you don't
like—which is being done—but this is a more subtle
way of doing it—to try to bring about discussions
and peace talks.

Q.

Jeff, what got you started with all this?

A.

Well, you know, one day I went home and my
daughter said Allie just got killed in Vietnam.
And Allie's her brother Allen—her little brother—
she's four and he's two and a half.

And she gets this from watching television.
And she relates to killing.
At four years old they take this.
And I guess she has nightmares about it.
I'm Jewish, you know. Not a practicing Jew, but I grew up most of my life dreaming about concentration camps—and I still do—and it's very frightening.
Like when I was young my wife's whole family got wiped out in Russia. They just killed the whole town. My father was very aware of these things. We had books and pictures and I've seen a lot of footage from archives and, you know, you see pictures like *The Pawnbroker* and I look at my kids and I can't imagine somebody coming into my house and taking my two kids out and bashing their heads against the wall as babies and there's no way to stop these people from doing it.

NOT AS YET DECIDED

Jeff Dell

1967

50 seconds, black and white, 16mm.

Purchase: $20.00
Rental: $7.00; in Canada $3.00 (#67)

Awards

Expo '67 Silver Medal

DODGE CITY

Jeff Dell

1967

4 minutes, black and white, 16mm.

Purchase: $60.00
Rental: $10.00; in Canada $5.00 (#67)

Awards

Awarded Prizes at the Festivals of
San Francisco and Locarno, Italy, 1967

HAPPY BIRTHDAY, FELISA

Jeff Dell

1968

10 minutes, color, 16mm.

Purchase: $135.00
Rental: $15.00

Awards

Silver Medal
Atlanta International Film Festival, 1968

REQUIEM

Jeff Dell

1968

4 minutes, color, 16mm.

Purchase: $60:00
Rental: $10.00

Purchase:

Jeff Dell
Anifilm Studios
1150 6th Avenue
New York, N.Y.
212 867 4290

Stan Brakhage

WINDOW WATER BABY MOVING

Window Water Baby Moving **is a documentary of Brakhage's wife Jane giving birth to their first child. With water and light imagery and the delicacy of his editing, Brakhage reaches an unusual level of poetry.** *Window Water Baby Moving* **is a silent film, but Brakhage conveys through the images of blood and pain a visual sense of the sacred which would be lessened by any soundtrack.** *Window Water Baby Moving* **ventures into a difficult area of human experience and succeeds.**

How did witnessing the birth affect you?

Did you share the feelings of the mother and father as you witnessed the birth?

Do you think the camera communicated some of the mystery and sacredness of childbirth?

Did the absence of sound add to or subtract from the film?

What do the following words mean to you after seeing this film: sex, abortion, love, a good lay, mother, playboy.

"People who worry about the moral danger of abortion do so because they think of the fetus as a human being. . . . Abortion prohibitionists generally insist that abortion is murder, and that an embryo is a person; but no state or nation, so far as I know, requires the dead fetus to be treated like a dead person. Although all of the states in the United States severely limit what can be done with a dead body, no cognizance is taken of dead fetuses up to about five months of prenatal life. The early fetus may, with impunity, be flushed down the toilet or thrown out with the garbage—which shows that we never have regarded it as a human being. Scientific analysis confirms what we have always known."

From "Abortion—Or Compulsory Pregnancy?" by Garrett Hardin, Journal of Marriage and the Family (*May, 1968*).

"A mother accepts her child before she knows who that child will be. As long as a mother is carrying her child, she cannot know its sex or the color of its eyes. She cannot know whether it will be strong and sturdy or weak and ailing, whether it will be a laughing baby or a sad and lonely one. Until it is born, she cannot know how intense its need for her will be or even whether it will live. She accepts on faith the child's coming into being and the child's identity, as yet unknown. Motherhood begins with this willingness to accept the unknown. . . . Each woman, knowing she is pregnant and knowing whose child she is carrying, must still be prepared, like her most primitive forebears, to cherish a being not yet known to her. And each woman is still left to ponder the mystery in her heart. Modern women are freed from the terrors of the unknown, the dangers of giving birth in the dark and the cold, the anxieties of meeting an infant's need for food—the worst difficulties that haunted the imagination of primitive women. But civilization confronts us with difficulties of our own making. . . . Yet the modern mother is still asked to love her child unconditionally, and the child now, as in the past, is dependent on her unconditional love. . . . The child whose mother has succeeded in giving it a sense of being valued as a unique individual, entirely for itself, without regard for the accidents of beauty or brains or special talent, is prepared as a person to meet the challenges of living. We do not know—man has never known—how else to give a human being a sense of selfhood and identity, a sense of the worth of the world, and abiding trust in human relationships. . . . The love and care a child evokes in its mother does not depend on whether it is beautiful or homely, plump or thin, fretful or content; as long as it lives—and, hopefully, thrives, it is hers to care for. It is this absolute, unconditional acceptance that every child needs. . . . For the child must go forth from the warmth and safety of its mother's care."

From Family, *Margaret Mead, pages 13–19.*

WINDOW WATER BABY MOVING

Stan Brakhage

1959

12 minutes, color, silent, 16mm.

Purchase: inquire (#20)
Rental: $15.00 (#14, #20)

Award

Brussels International Film Festival, 1964

Ed Emshwiller   THANATOPSIS

Emshwiller is recognized as one of the best film technicians in the underground, and *Thanatopsis* **is perhaps his most technically impressive work. His films are precision planned and executed.** *Thanatopsis,* **for example, was photographed by single-frame time exposure. In** *Thanatopsis,* **the figure of a woman dances eerily around the head of a man, effecting a study of tension and anxiety. Emshwiller combines a constant heartbeat and the noise of a buzzsaw for his soundtrack.**

Is there a theme in Thanatopsis?

What mood does Emshwiller create in Thanatopsis?

How does he create this mood?

What does the title "Thanatopsis" mean to you?

Why does the lady change the color of her dress in the film?

Do you think Emshwiller has gained anything by his special technique in making this film?

50 PATIENTS STARVE TO DEATH

MONTEVIDEO (Reuters)—At least 50 patients at a mental home near here died of malnutrition in June and July, Public Health Minister Walter Ravenna admits. An inquiry is being conducted into conditions at the home.

INDIA MONSOONS KILL 6 CHILDREN

NEW DELHI (Reuters)—Monsoon rains in West Bengal—the worst in 50 years—have killed six children and submerged 1,000 square miles, reports reaching here said today.

THE WAR DEAD

WASHINGTON (AP)—The names of 111 men killed in action are on the latest Defense Dept. casualty list from Vietnam.

N.Y. Post, August 27, 1968

COMPTON, Cal. (AP)—A helicopter carrying children and adults from Los Angeles to Disneyland

exploded in a fireball over a playground today and police said its 21 occupants were killed.

N.Y. Post, August 14, 1968

THANATOLOGY

Although the Sydney assembly could not agree on a precise definition of death, there is now a virtually world-wide consensus on the following criteria for establishing that irreversible coma, or death, has indeed occurred:

1. Total lack of response to external stimuli, even the most painful that can ethically be applied.

2. Absence of all spontaneous muscular movements, notably breathing. If the patient is on a mechanical respirator, this may be turned off for three minutes in order to establish that he is incapable of breathing for himself.

3. Absence of reflexes. The dilated pupils must not contract when a bright light is shone directly into them. There must be no eye movements in response to pouring ice water into the ears, no muscular contractions after hammer-tapping the tendons of the biceps, triceps or quadriceps.

4. Flat encephalogram or absence of "brain waves."

Significantly, the heart received least attention from the thanatologists. Both the difficulty and the urgency of their task resulted largely from the fact that a heart-lung machine can keep major parts of a body "alive" long after effective death. The long-held notion that death can be pinpointed in time, four or five minutes after heart action and breathing have stopped, is erroneous, said Cleveland's Dr. Charles L. Hudson, principal U.S. delegate in Sydney.

"Death," Hudson said, "is a gradual process at the cellular level, with tissues varying in their ability to withstand deprivation of oxygen. Medical interest, however, lies not in the preservation of isolated cells but in the fate of a person. Here the point of death is not so important as the certainty that the process has become irreversible."

Time, August 16, 1968

THANATOPSIS

So live, that, when thy summons comes to join
The innumerable caravan, that moves
To that mysterious realm, where each shall take
His chamber in the silent halls of death,
Thou go not, like the quarry-slave, at night,
Scourged to his dungeon, but, sustain'd and soothed
By an unfaltering trust, approach thy grave,
Like one that draws the drapery of his couch
About him, and lies down to pleasant dreams.

William Cullen Bryant

THANATOPSIS

Ed Emshwiller

1962

5 minutes, black and white, 16mm.

Purchase: inquire (#20)
Rental: $6.00 (#20, #14)

Award

Special recognition for technical excellence
Third International Experimental Film Festival
Belgium, 1963–64

Peter Gessner TIME OF THE LOCUST

Time of the Locust is a statement by Peter Gessner about the Vietnam war. It includes National Liberation Front footage, the work of Japanese camera units, and American newsfilm. Gessner attempts to move the Vietnam war from the level of law or military strategy to the level of individual people. In *Time of the Locust* **pain becomes more important than politics.**

How can Americans come to know the real truth about the war in Vietnam and particularly those aspects of the war presented in this film?

To what extent should persons of national authority expect to be held accountable for the facts and the deeds that lie back of policy statements and public pronouncements? To what extent must every citizen share responsibility along with the President for U.S. actions in Vietnam?

Does exposure of violence and brutality serve a useful purpose? Can we honestly face ourselves and this aspect of our Vietnam involvement?

How can American citizens meet their responsibilities for the situation in Vietnam? What changes in policy are needed? What can be done to bring them about?

When, in a highly complex situation, brutality and violence get the upper hand (and this is commonly the case in any war), it is easy for the people themselves to become brutalized by what is going on on all sides. Equally dangerous is escapism which simply denies the evil that exists. Either way, apathy is the result, and apathy is a form of moral surrender and defeat. Do you agree?

News reports out of Saigon on the night of December 12, 1965, told of 23 Vietnamese civilians massacred by the Viet Cong. They were sprayed by machine gun fire as they slept. Seven others were critically wounded, and among the survivors was a three-year-old child, found under the dead body of its mother.

Their crime? They had been working on a canal for a small village south of Saigon. The Viet Cong did not want that canal built, and a finger on the trigger of a machine gun was their way of resolving the problem.

On October 3, a blast occurred at 1:15 in the afternoon outside Cong Hoa Stadium, where policemen had been going through training exercises. Nine persons—five policemen and four children—were killed, and thirty-two persons were injured. A second explosive device, discovered concealed in a basket of vegetables, was dismantled. Another explosion occurred later in the day at another place in the city. A bomb or grenade being transported in a taxi exploded, apparently prematurely. Two people were killed and ten others injured.

On August 24, 1964, a well-dressed Viet Cong registered under a false name at Saigon's Caravelle Hotel. He was given a room on the fifth floor. The following day left the hotel, and a few minutes later an explosion rocked the building. The Caravelle is one of Saigon's international spots, and the Viet Cong were evidently hoping to kill Americans. No Americans were killed or injured. However, one Frenchman, one New Zealander, and more than a dozen Vietnamese were wounded.

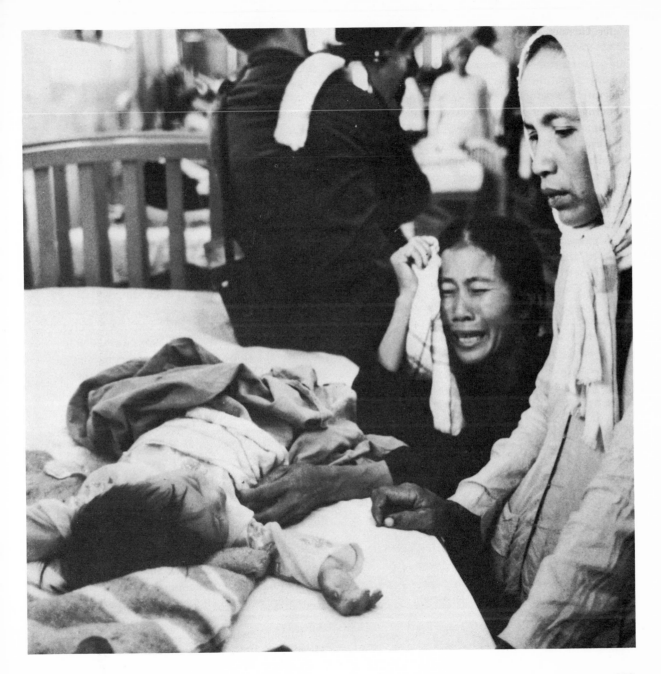

There are many phases to the Vietnamese terror-blocking program in the cities. The following are among the more important steps that have been taken:

1. "Resources control," i.e., cutting off Viet Cong resources and movements. At roads leading into Saigon, police at checkpoints search vehicles to make sure that explosives are not being smuggled into the city. In the city itself, white-uniformed police on various streets spot-check passing cars: for example, every fifth or every tenth car is stopped and searched, and its occupants asked to show identification papers. A census is conducted frequently in an effort to keep track of the persons living in an area; an unexplained "cousin" from the interior would be suspect as a possible Viet Cong.

2. There are nine precincts in Saigon, and in each one a "sweep" is carried out nightly. The police block off an area, then examine every square foot of it, seeking Viet Cong, criminals, and anyone else caught in the net. Depending on the size of the area being searched, anywhere from 50 to 1000 police participate, and in at least one case 1400 police were used.

3. The Saigon police utilize routine police intelligence techniques. They get tips from informants, they give out rewards, and they have occasionally succeeded in penetrating the Viet Cong apparatus with their own spies.

4. Normal police investigative techniques are used.

THE LOCUST SWARM

Locusts laid their eggs in the corpse
Of a soldier. When the worms were
Mature, they took wing. Their drone
Was ominous, their shells hard.
Anyone could tell they had hatched
From an unsatisfied anger.
They flew swiftly towards the North.
They hid the sky like a curtain.
When the wife of the soldier
Saw them, she turned pale, her breath
Failed her. She knew he was dead
In battle, his corpse lost in
The desert. That night she dreamed
She rode a white horse, so swift
It left no footprints, and came
To where he lay in the sand.
She looked at his face, eaten
By the locusts, and tears of
Blood filled her eyes. Ever after
She would not let her children
Injure any insect which
Might have fed on the dead. She
Would lift her face to the sky
And say, "O locusts, if you
Are seeking a place to winter,
You can find shelter in my heart."

TIME OF THE LOCUST

Peter Gessner

1966

12 minutes, black and white, 16mm.

Purchase: inquire (#1, #20); in Canada (#68)
Rental: $15.00 (#1, #20); in Canada (#68)

Awards

Mannheim, 1966

Leipzig, 1966
Tours, 1967
Festival dei Populi, 1967
Invited Film, 1966, Robert Flaherty International
Film Seminar

Guvnor Nelson and Dorothy Wiley

SCHMEERGUNTZ

    **Guvnor Nelson and Dorothy Wiley, the wives
of two noted underground filmmakers, satirize
modern woman and uncover the false glamor
perpetuated by advertising and the mass media.
Nelson and Wiley contrast the polished face of
television behind which nothing is ever dirty or ugly
with the non-salacious nudity of a woman in the
final stages of pregnancy and the unromantic secrets
of housecleaning and infant care. Toilet imagery is
dominant.**
    **According to Mrs. Nelson and Mrs. Wiley,
"Schmeerguntz" is a nonsense word that represents
how a Swede imagines what a sandwich would be
called in German.**

*Do you think advertising has a beneficial effect on
what persons think of themselves, on how the individual forms his personal value-system, and on
what people consider beauty?*

*How do you grow in awareness of your own personal
identity so that the powerful forces of advertising
do not dilute or mutilate your self-image?*

*Do you recognize the real motives that commercials
and ads appeal to? In what way do you learn to
evaluate such solicitation?*

*Create an advertisement which tries to sell a product
by appealing to "glamor" motives.*

*Do you think that the strong imagery in this film
succeeds?*

*How would different community audiences react to
this film—for example, a parish men's club and a
PTA meeting?*

    "Who knows where you draw a line between
comedy and tragedy? Take a funeral, for instance:
the most solemn occasion. Everyone in black; tears,
flowers, handkerchiefs. And then a little man arrives
rather late, very breathless. He sneaks into church
and sits down beside a very fat mourner who gives
him a perishing look. Nervously, he moves up a
seat and sits on somebody's hat. In no time, it's an
hilarious comedy."
    "Then there's the gag about the man who goes
to a very pompous dinner party. Everything goes
wrong for him. The butler gets his name wrong; his
neighbor at table drops butter on his coat; the
serving maid pours soup down his neck. He suffers
it all with a smile and polite reassurances: 'Oh,
please don't bother—it's quite all right.' Then, finally,
after the last indignity, he goes berserk, runs wildly
round the room, breaking the china, scaring the
guests, and, at last, setting fire to the place." For a
moment, Chaplin was lost in visions of happy
anarchy.

Charles Chaplin, Interviews With Film Directors, *ed. Andrew
Sarris (New York, 1967), page 66.*

SCHMEERGUNTZ

Guvnor Nelson
Dorothy Wiley

1966

15 minutes, 16 mm.

Purchase: inquire (#20)
Rental: $15.00 (#4, #11, #20); in Canada
(#71)

Awards

Ann Arbor Film Festival, 1966, Webster College
Film Festival, Chicago Art Center Festival,
Milwaukee Film Festival

Andy Warhol SAMPLER

Sampler **includes short clips from four Andy
Warhol films:** *Sleep, Eat, Haircut* **and** *Empire.*
Sleep, **at feature length, is a six-hour study of a man
sleeping. It seems to be an attempt by Warhol to
apply the spirit of pop art to filmmaking. Warhol
confronts the viewer with the simple act of a man
sleeping over a long period of time. The slightest
change in the sleeping man's posture becomes an
event of major interest. In this way, the ordinary
experience of sleep is presented to the viewer in a
new way as if for the first time. For those who wish
to be warned, there is a slight hint of pubic hair
throughout.**

Eat, **at full length, is a 45-minute study of a man
eating a mushroom;** *Haircut,* **at full length, is a 33-
minute study of a man receiving a haircut; and**
Empire, **at feature length, is an eight-hour study of
the Empire State Building.**

From the *Daily News,* June 4, 1968, p. 3.

As part of news coverage on the critical
gunshot wounding of Andy Warhol by one of
his female stars, the New York Daily News had
this to say about his life and work:

After squirming through 3½ hours of Andy
Warhol's underground epic, "The Chelsea Girls,"
one critic labeled it "a tragedy full of desperation,
hardness, and terror." After 36 years of squirming
through a world whose values he rejected as jaded,
Andy Warhol may have come to regard his life in
similar terms.

Warhol, who took such utilitarian objects as
Brillo pads and Campbell soup cans out of the
kitchen and moved them into the living room in the
guise of pop art, recognized that there was gold to
be mined in pandering to the hang-ups and fetishes
of people. He coined a mint out of the very decadence
to which he contributed.

Like One of His Scripts

The tragedy which unfolded in his office yesterday doubtless hurt Warhol a lot more than it
shocked him. The real-life drama had some of the
characteristics of his underground films. The sex,
the violence, the plotlessness—avante—ingredients,
all of them.

In a sense, what happened yesterday digressed
from the usual Warhol script only to a small extent.
Persons like Warhol just don't go getting into deep
trouble in the businesslike atmosphere of an office.
Their crises are usually resolved or dissolved in
more intimate locales—or in some Tennessee Williams setting, at least.

Psychedelia and all its vague manifestations
permeated Warhol's films. How else can you explain
a film in which the star (and total supporting cast)
is the Empire State Building. Yet thousands sat for

eight hours to watch a film whose total attention was focused on the world's tallest skyscraper.

Another of his films ran for six hours and was devoted to a man sleeping, just sleeping. There was a lot more animation in his next film. It showed a man eating a mushroom—a fast-paced 45 minutes of symbolism.

Some called Warhol the Peter Pan of Pop Art. Others were less kind as they exited from his screenings scratching their perplexed heads.

Sex and Sin His Staples

When Warhol took the time and bother to aim at something, one of his favorite targets was invariably the so-called "establishment." Its emphasis on such accessories of life as money bugged Warhol.

Oddly, he had a thing about silver. There was a time when everything about him had to be painted silver, including his hi-fi set and the hair on his head. This made for lots of unrehearsed dialog between himself and his coterie of fans, friends and hangers-on.

Then, most of the lines about all that silver got to be predictable and Warhol went and changed things. Under stress, he could innovate.

But in his films, even when he tried to be different, Warhol scored his biggest successes selling some of tired old world's most familiar commodities —sex and sin, sin and sex. He gave them co-billing.

Warhol's family originally came from a little town near Prague in Czechoslovakia. The family emigrated to the United States and settled in Pittsburgh.

After grade-school, young Andy studied art at Carnegie Tech. He moved to New York and took up pop art in the early '50s.

Warhol, born Aug. 8, 1931, in Cleveland, achieved fame with his paintings depicting the Campbell soup can. He has had one-man art shows here, at the Leo Castelli and Stable Galleries, and in Los Angeles, Toronto, Buenos Aires and Paris. In 1964 he received the Sixth Film Culture Award and the Los Angeles Film Festival award.

SAMPLER

Andy Warhol

1963–1965

4 minutes, black and white, silent, 16mm.

Purchase: inquire (#20)
Rental: $20.00 (#20)

Stan Vanderbeek   SCIENCE FRICTION

Stan Vanderbeek is a master of animated collage and has developed an ideal film form for satire. Paradoxical magazine images clash together. Objects change their shape and meaning at rapid speed. Unlikely symbols are likely to be found out of traditional order.

Science Friction satirizes technology and the space age. It was compiled from great quantities of footage photographed over several years and is an example of Vanderbeek's "sausage" method of making a film—cut off at the end when finished.

Name fifteen major images in Science Friction.

How does Vanderbeek manipulate these images to achieve satire?

Discuss five major images and attempt to discover how many times they occur and in what contexts.

Scene from *Science Friction*

How many times in one minute does an image change?

Do you feel that you would be able to make a film like Science Friction? *Pick a topic and plan one.*

Up to now, the vast majority of avant-garde films have been crudely made jumbles, pornographic psychodramas, interesting failures or imperfect successes. But Mekas[1] believes the underground has passed the larval stage and is ready to furnish the public with intelligent, independent films Hollywood neglects.

"Underground cinema started from scratch, like a dirty boy," explains Mekas, a Lithuanian refugee who attended a showing of *The Cabinet of Dr. Caligari* the night he set foot in New York in 1949. "The new cinema even used dirty words. It hated its parents. It landed in jail. Now it still has pimples on its face and it still makes mistakes. But it refuses to undergo Hollywood plastic surgery to correct them. It will only be a matter of 3 or 4 years before a great many theaters will take underground films for commercial distribution." "Our best moviemakers used to make $300 or $400 a year from film rentals," says Mekas. "Now they make from $3,000 to $6,000."

From "Up from the Underground," Newsweek, April 25, 1966, page 90.

To the question asked about the goal of my film, I would be able thus to reply: "I want to be one of the artists of the cathedral that rises on the plain. I want to occupy myself by carving out of stone the head of a dragon, an angel or a demon, or perhaps a saint; it doesn't matter; I will find the same joy

[1] *Jonas Mekas is one of the directors of Filmmakers' Co-op and writes for the* Village Voice.

in any case. Whether I am a believer or an unbeliever, Christian or pagan, I work with all the world to build a cathedral because I am artist and artisan, and because I have learned to draw faces, limbs, and bodies out of stone. I will never worry about the judgment of posterity or of my contemporaries; my name is carved nowhere and will disappear with me. But a little part of myself will survive in the anonymous and triumphant totality. A dragon or a demon, or perhaps a saint, it doesn't matter!"

Ingmar Bergman, Interviews with Film Directors, *ed. Andrew Sarris (New York, 1967), page 22.*

SCIENCE FRICTION

Stan Vanderbeek

1959

9 minutes, color, 16mm./35mm.

Purchase: inquire (#20, #14)
Rental: $9.00 (#20, #14)

Awards

Award of Distinction, Creative Film Foundation
Highest Award, West German and Bergamo
International Film Festivals
Selected for special presentation at the Museum of Modern Art.

PROPAGANDA FILMS

TRIUMPH OF THE WILL (*40-minute version*)
NAZI STRIKE
THE BATTLE OF SAN PIETRO

It is difficult to assess the significance of propaganda films. Are their distortions legitimate? Are they legitimate if executed with a high degree of film art? Are they legitimate if their purpose is to lead people ultimately to truth? How do they relate to the use of images in advertising? How do they relate to the use of images in highly symbolic commercial filmmaking—for example, *Two Men and a Wardrobe* (**cf. p. 52**)? Does the distortion of reality involved in any of these forms contribute to communication? How involved is the Church with propaganda? Is *Hunger in America* propaganda (**cf. p. 67**)? Since these questions pertain to human freedom and communication, three related propaganda films are included here from the most propagandized period of our history.

TRIUMPH OF THE WILL is the official German film report of the 6th Nazi Party Congress held at Nurenberg, Sept. 4th to 10th, 1934. It was created by Leni Riefenstahl at the order of Adolf Hitler to be "a display of political power for millions of Germans." Its purpose was to justify the Nazi way of acting and to introduce the German people, in Germany and all over the world, to unknown Nazi figures such as Rudolf Hess and Heinrich Himmler. Riefenstahl moved into the Congress with 19 cameramen and 21 assistants, practically transforming it into a movie set. After a year of editing, Riefenstahl produced what is perhaps the most brilliant propaganda film in history.

NAZI STRIKE is part of the World War II American *Why We Fight* series. In 1943 Bosley Crowther described the series: "They were made to show, progressively, the factors behind the present war and the nature of the enemy's aggression—and the resistance to it—during the first desperate years" (*New York Times,* **Nov. 15**). *Nazi Strike* recounts the first years of Nazi aggression and lives up to the most stereotyped expectations of propaganda films. It compares Hitler, for example, to a distorted cartoon face of Genghis Khan. *Nazi Strike* fails most fundamentally, moreover, in its attempt to tell the German story with Nazi footage, particularly when borrowed from *Triumph of the Will.* **The narrator speaks with such enthusiasm that the Nazi film becomes more inspiring than horrifying.** *Nazi Strike* is difficult to take seriously, but it is a clear example of propaganda, and since it includes footage from *Triumph of the Will,* **is makes an excellent companion piece to that film.**

THE BATTLE OF SAN PIETRO is an American film about the capture of San Pietro in Italy by Fifth Army forces. San Pietro was the military key to an important valley. The ability of the Fifth Army to control this valley would contribute significantly to the Allied position in Italy and would engage a large number of enemy troops. *The Battle of San Pietro* **is included here because it is about American rather than Nazi forces and it complements the picture of World War II propaganda given by** *Triumph of the Will* **and** *Nazi Strike.*

How do the Mormon Tabernacle Choir and the St. Brendan's Boys' Choir contribute to the story of San Pietro?

What use is made of the church of San Pietro and of religion in general?

Are the American dead handled differently than the enemy dead?

Was the American soldier in World War II always smiling and fully equipped?

Did Nazi or American bombardment destroy the church and the buildings of San Pietro?

Toward the conclusion of the film, the American forces are portrayed more as the liberators of Italy than as a simple military ploy to engage enemy troops. Is this change justified?

TRIUMPH OF THE WILL

Leni Riefenstahl, UFA

1935

40 minutes—English titles
2 hours—no titles
black and white, 16mm.

Purchase: inquire (#31)
Rental: $30.00–$60.00 (#31); in Canada (#68)

Directed and edited by Leni Riefenstahl

NAZI STRIKE

Lieut. Col. Frank Capra, War Dept.
Maj. Anatole Lituak

1943

58 minutes, black and white, 16mm.

Purchase: inquire (#31); in Canada (#68)
Rental: $20.00–$40.00 (#31); in Canada (#68)

Script by Capt. Anthony Veiller
Photography by Corp. Robert Hiller

THE BATTLE OF SAN PIETRO

U.S. Army Pictorial Service

1944

30 minutes, black and white, 16mm.

Purchase: inquire (#31); in Canada $60.00 (#68)
Rental: $12.00–$24.00 (#31); in Canada $7.50–$10.00 (#68)

Produced by Army Pictorial Services
Directed by Maj. John Houston
Photographed by Capt. Jules Buck & Signal Corps cameramen

FEATURE FILMS
RELATED TO DISCOVERY THEMES

Communication
The Miracle Worker
David and Lisa
The Silence
Nobody Waved Goodbye
Cat on a Hot Tin Roof
Blackboard Jungle
The Mark
Through a Glass Darkly
The Winter Light
Le Bonheur
The Battle of the Sexes

Freedom
Open City
Animal Farm
The Loneliness of the Long Distance Runner
A Man for All Seasons
Zorba the Greek
A Raisin in the Sun
Cry, the Beloved Country
On the Waterfront
To Kill a Mockingbird
Cool World
The Connection
Nothing but a Man

Love
A Taste of Honey
The Girl with Green Eyes
Darling
Sundays and Cybele
The Spy Who Came In from the Cold
Marty
The Virgin Spring
Alfie

Breakfast at Tiffany's
Dimka
A Man and A Woman
Jules and Jim
The L-Shaped Room
The Quiet One
The Collector

Peace
Hiroshima, Mon Amour
King of Hearts
How I Won the War
On the Beach
Dr. Strangelove
No Greater Love
The Victors
For King and Country
The Ballad of a Soldier
The Cranes Are Flying
The Shop on Main Street

Happiness
Nights of Cabiria
Chaplin
La Strada
The Seventh Seal
La Dolce Vita
Grapes of Wrath
Death of a Salesman
The Old Man and the Sea
Wild Strawberries
Room at the Top
Life at the Top
The Diary of Ann Frank
The Brink of Life
The Pawnbroker
East of Eden

TEACHING THE FILM

College and high school students, grammar school children—even pre-school children—are getting involved with filmmaking. And many educators have taken the stand that film art has become a necessary study. Two suggestions are offered in this essay: a film course based on the films discussed in this book and the idea of a film "term paper."

Film "term papers," or film essays, have been initiated in various schools and organizations with great success. Students seem to take a new interest in curriculum subject matter when they are told to make a serious statement about it in film. Parochial schools and religious study groups will find that theology lends itself well to an experiment of this nature. Shooting a film about poverty, for example, not only gives the student facts, but also creates in him the ability to understand a significant human problem with more than usual empathy.

A film term paper is possible in most schools without extraordinary preparation. Eight millimeter film and processing are within the price range of most students, particularly if the expenses are shared by a film group of four or five members. One-fourth to one-fifth of a normal class of high school students has access to an eight millimeter camera through family or friends. A twelve-dollar eight millimeter film editor can be purchased to aid in film splicing, and an eight millimeter projector can be borrowed from one of the camera owners.

At the beginning of the term paper assignment, the class should divide into groups of four or five, with a camera owner included in every group. Practical details should be decided in small group discussion: topic of paper, budget, rough scenario, exchange of telephone numbers, work time and shooting location.

A ten-minute instruction in the art of filmmaking may be given by the teacher, more for the psychological security of the students than for any practical reason. Students are fascinated with the synthetic nature of filmmaking and have responded well to the following ideas: How does a filmmaker say "door opening" in film language? Is it a question of fixing a camera steadily on a door while it opens? The filmmaker mixes his shots—doorknob shot, medium shot of door, shot of door angled down from a ladder, etc. He breaks down his film object —door—and its action—opening—into component visual elements, and then pieces them together again by an editing process in order to recreate in film language the experience of "door opening." The filmmaker, moreover, usually states something beyond "door opening." Through his selectivity of shots, he develops an emotional context for the door opening. Doors open in mystery stories, war stories, musical comedies and slapstick. How does a door open suspensefully? A filmmaker might emphasize shadow shots and looming upward angle shots. Film art, therefore, minimally involves a breakdown of any object, action, emotion or theme into component elements and an editing process which reunites them.

Editing is the secret of any good film. Students should plan money and time for editing. They should buy more film than they think they will need and allot as much time to rearranging the film from its original shooting order as they spend on the actual shooting. A hand-turned editor-viewer, a splicer, and a seventy-nine cent packet of splicing tape are all the materials necessary.

Sound contributes greatly to a film. Although eight millimeter film cannot carry a soundtrack directly on its surface, it is possible to make a tape-recorded soundtrack for simultaneous playback with the film. Exact synchronization is not advisable in this situation, but the process can be used for a general background soundtrack. Two to three months is a good amount of time to allow for a film term paper assignment.

The film term paper, however, does not necessarily communicate a developed sense of film art to the student. It may be desirable to establish a film course exclusively for this purpose. It is possible to base such a course on a study of non-feature films such as those included in this book.

For school and organizational scheduling, a feature film with time for discussion is difficult to arrange with the regularity demanded by a film course. A second showing of a feature film is usually impossible. Moreover, novice film viewers do not have ninety minutes of analytical attention to devote to a film, and they find it difficult to recall ninety minutes of film data with accuracy and detail. It is also easier to find high quality non-feature films, particularly on a high school level, than to maintain a high level of quality in a list of ten or fifteen feature films.

Many of the non-feature films included in this book are available free of charge to groups and organizations for non-classroom showings through public library systems. In school situations, the English and Theology departments may be willing to share film costs with the Film department for films of mutual interest. The film course outlined here was designed for one semester: thirty eighty-minute periods: fifteen teaching periods, fifteen film-making workshop periods. This course, as it was actually taught at Regis High School in New York City, cost the Film department twenty-seven dollars. The fifteen teaching periods:

1. **Vivre; A Trumpeter for the Combo.**
   Purpose:

To elicit from the students the different elements of film art—types of shots, editing, sequential division of a film, sound, the filmmaker's particular style, etc. To begin to train the students to recall the exact images in a film. Every student comment should have an exact reference to something in the text of the film. The students should at first take notes while keeping their eyes fixed on the screen; a simple list of images can stimulate recall of a good portion of any non-feature film.

2. "Homecoming Scene" sequence from **Birth of a Nation** (Museum of Modern Art); **The Soldier; Sky.**
   Purpose:
   To discuss the synthetic nature of film art; how film art breaks down an object, action or theme into component elements and edits them together within the limits of film language. "Homecoming Scene" is a primitive example of film art and contrasts well with the more sophisticated techniques in **The Soldier** and **Sky.**

3. **An Occurrence at Owl Creek Bridge.** Two showings: the second with stop action and running commentary.
   Purpose:
   To discuss the standard camera shots, camera angles, camera motions. Many specific shots in **An Occurrence at Owl Creek Bridge** are mentioned in the full discussion of the film earlier in this book.

4. "Odessa Steps" sequence from **Battleship Potemkin** (Museum of Modern Art); **Night and Fog.**
   Purpose:
   To discuss editing or montage. It might be well to note here the significance of Sergei Eisenstein **(Battleship Potemkin)** to editing and to film art in general. Information about Eisen-

stein and an explanation of concepts of film theory and film production helpful to this course are available in **Film World** (Penguin, 1967).

5. **Two Men and a Wardrobe.** Two showings: the second showing with stop action and running commentary.
Purpose:
To discuss the composition of a sequence and the relationship of sequence to sequence within a film. Each sequence of **Two Men and a Wardrobe** is listed with questions in the full discussion of the film earlier in this book.

6. **400 Blows** (Janus Films), a feature film.
Purpose:
To discuss the feature film as compared to the short film; the relationship of sequence to sequence over a longer period of time.

7. **The Game.**
Purpose:
To review classes three, four, and five.

8. **Lines Horizontal; Television Commercials.**
Purpose:
To discuss symbolism and the psychological impact of an image.

9. **Triumph of the Will** (40-minute version); **23 Skidoo; Schmeerguntz.**
Purpose:
To discuss the psychological impact of an image in the context of propaganda and the "art" film. It might be well to require a written essay from the students about the films in classes eight and nine.

10. **String Bean; Adventures of an*; Leaf**
Purpose:
To discuss the use of color. It would be helpful to recall the use of color in **Night and Fog** and **Lines Horizontal.**

11. **Very Nice, Very Nice; My Own Back Yard To Play In; The Critic; Window Water Baby Moving.**
Purpose:
To discuss the use of sound. It would be helpful to recall the use of sound in "Odessa Steps" sequence, **An Occurrence at Owl Creek Bridge, The Game,** and **Triumph of the Will.**

12. **The Seventh Seal** (Janus Films), a feature film.
Purpose:
To apply classes eight and nine to the feature film.

13. Student-Made films.
Purpose:
To give the class a sense of accomplishment and to review the concepts of the course as embodied in their own work.

14. **A Divided World.** Two showings
Purpose:
Final examination. The students should write a forty-minute essay analyzing **Divided World** in the light of the entire course.

15. Student-Made films.
Purpose:
Party atmosphere. Draw extra electricity into the workshop room and run ten projectors at once. Experiment with mirrors and jells and spontaneously constructed projection surfaces.

RETREAT WORK AND THE FILM

A "retreat" is a time of prayer, reflection and renewal. Films have frequently been used during times of retreat to encourage new awareness, and many of the films discussed in this book can be related to traditional areas of retreat concern. Twenty-three films are included in this list of retreat suggestions. Their order of presentation was determined by the *Spiritual Exercises* of Ignatius Loyola.

THEME	FILM
Man's purpose on earth	**Inscape, The Hand, Time Piece.**
Self-examination: teenagers and personal relations; teenagers and parents; social conscience.	**The Game, Phoebe. David and Hazel, No Reason To Stay. Hunger in America, Interview with Bruce Gordon, Schmeerguntz, Very Nice, Very Nice.**
Evil and sin, man at his worst.	**Night and Fog, Two Men and a Wardrobe.**
Birth of Christ.	**Christmas in Appalachia.**
Life of Christ.	**Gandhi, Interview with Bruce Gordon, Roadsigns on a Merry-Go-Round.**
Good vs. evil, Christ vs. not-Christ.	**The Most** and **In the Name of God** shown together.
Commitment.	**Triumph of the Will** and **Viva La Calle 103** shown together.
Death of Christ.	**Hunger in America, Night and Fog, The Soldier**
New birth, God's love.	**Overture, Window Water Baby Moving.**

ALPHABETICAL INDEX OF FILMS

7